# THE KINGDOM

## *of* HEAVEN *is* Like

Dr. Don D. Hughes

# CONTENTS

# DEDICATION AND MEMORIAL

I WOULD LIKE TO dedicate *The Kingdom Parables*, my fourth book, to one of my spiritual fathers, Bishop Vernon D. Owens (1951-2006). He passed on to his reward on July 3, 2006. Our paths first crossed in 1986 as he was pastoring in Merced, California, and I had just begun pioneering a new work in Stockton, California. We met at a ministers' meeting and almost instantly became great friends. We ministered together, as well as in each other's churches. We played golf (and I might add quite regularly), spent vacations days together and spoke weekly to each other on the phone.

Bishop was one of the first real Holy Ghost preachers I had met that actually had substance in his high-volume preaching. I'll never forget the first time I heard him preach; it seemed like the place was electric as he brought forth God's Word. I began my ministry during the Word of Faith movement, whose truths were mainly taught through teachers and pastors. My own father, Dr. Don Hughes, Sr., (one of God's leaders in that movement) taught me how to present God's word, line upon line, and precept (Isa. 28:10).

Bishop Owens unveiled before me the anointed preaching of prophetic truth. He was one of the first ministers in my life that brought the kingdom into view. He loved the Word of God, the moved of the Holy Ghost and preachers, mercy oozed from his very pores. He was the first minister who contacted me and believed that I was worth restoring. There was a season I was privileged to travel with him in his itinerant ministry. I served him, drove him to his meetings, ironed his clothes and got him his favorite McDonald's coffee (I'm not sure how anyone could like that coffee, but Dad Owens loved it).

In the hotel rooms preparing for a meeting, I saw him pray with passion, and in the meetings, it was nothing for him to pray for everybody in the building, prophesying the Word of the Lord over many. I say him slap oil and throw water on entire congregations. He taught me how to be sensitive to the Holy Spirit. I *caught* several things from him, including the power of preaching present-day truth from the stories of the Bible, using illustrations from television, and even how to preach prophetic truth from today's headlines of the newspaper (He use to hand me the newspaper and say "pick a headline, a phrase and I can develop a message from it." Sometimes he would have me pick a verse from the Bible, any verse and preach a message right on the spot to me. Needless to say; there were times we laughed until we cried). His love for my children and I was unconditional. God used him to deliver me from the face of men and to dare to step out in the apostolic calling God had placed on my life. He unlocked and challenged the prophetic ministry that had always been inside of me, yet hidden among past hurts, inhibitions and the fear of what people thought.

When I started Impact Church in Charlotte (September 2000), he came on more than one occasion and spoke into the life of our young church, always encouraging me in the ministry. He had approached a few ministers, including myself, about the hunger in Korea for prophetic ministry and asked me to go with him to speak in several churches. While there ministering with my father in the Lord, out of my own ignorance and immaturity I pulled away from him upon returned to Charlotte.

It was only a month before his passing that I was given his number by a friend and re-connected with him. He was so Christ-like in his actions and conversation with me. He treated me as though I had never left, and we laughed and reminisced about old times. A few weeks late, he went into a coma, and then shortly after that, he was gone. He truly was one of my fathers in the faith. Men and women of God, ministers of the Gospel, please hear my heart. Let's put away childish things; let's understand the importance of "fathering" ministry. If you have run from them, run back to them. Life is too short, and you don't want to live your life with regrets.

In closing, Dad, I love you, Sir, and will forever be grateful for your example of your love for the Lord. Mom Therese, your children, grandchildren and myself. I will miss your laugh, our late-night snack of "Captain Crunch" cereal, and playing golf together. I'm sure our next conversation will be most interesting.

Forever your son,

# FOREWORDS

I GREW UP LISTENING to my father, Apostle Don Hughes, preach, teach, minister and prophesy to thousands of people all over the U.S. and abroad. I have watched his mindsets and foundations be challenged by the revelations God has made known to him through his studies. I have witnessed firsthand the struggles and tragedies he has overcome in his life and ministry. I stand firmly by my conviction that those who have been through hell in their lives, and yet don't quit, have a stronger anointing and a deeper understanding (revelation) of God's truth.

I had the privilege of hearing my father teach this series, "The Kingdom Parables," when it first was revealed to him. The revelation and insights that the Holy Spirit revealed to him are most profound. Apostle Don Hughes (Dad) has a unique ability to captivate your attention, break down the words and message from its original language and place you right into the story/parable.

Over the years, I have had the opportunity to hear an abundance of great men/women of God teach and preach truths that God has revealed to them. I can honestly say without hesitation, even though he is my father, Apostle Don Hughes is still my favorite. There is just something about his insight, his Hughes paraphrase (his breakdown of a word/verses origin) that is so captivating.

I know you have been blessed by his insight and through his God-given revelation in this book *The Kingdom Parables*.

Humbly,

*Donnie*

Donald "Donnie" Dewayne Hughes

MUCH OF THE Body of Christ has been a crossroad for some time now. Many still seem stuck in old religious mindsets: others are sitting in buildings worshiping past movements that are now monuments to past moves of God. And yet, there are even others who have left, strayed away from church due to hurts and wounds imposed upon them by other church members, friends and even family. I trust the truths revealed in the pages that you have just read have moved you from your disappointment, frustration and hurt, causing you to follow the cloud of God, to get back into the race (if you ever left) and allow the oil and wine of God's spirit to revive you.

Dad's book *The Kingdom Parables* takes these parables that we have read or heard preached hundreds of time over the years and breaks them down, showing us a better, fresh understanding of what they were meant to teach us. I can tell you that in my short thirty-seven years (as of 2018), that my father, Apostle Don Hughes, is one of the best preacher/teachers that I have ever heard.

His right now Rhema Word on these kingdom parables is one of the best series that I have ever heard him teach. He teaches these in such a way that everyone, no matter how long you have been in Christianity, you can understand them and receive new insight in your life.

Now that you have finished reading/studying these parables, you have been blessed, and are now walking with a fresh and new understanding of them. This book is great for everyone, from the new believer to the seasoned saints.

Sincerely,

*Kevin*

Kevin Matthew Hughes

# INTRODUCTION

T HE FOUR GOSPELS (Matthew, Mark, Luke, & John) record fifty-one different parables that Jesus taught during His earthly ministry. Of those fifty-one parables, only twelve begin with the statement, "the kingdom of heaven is like." I find it quite interesting that there are twelve. The number twelve (12) in Biblical numeric is a Kingdom number. It represents DIVINE GOVERNMENT, divine administration, and the elective purposes of God.

What exactly is a parable? The word *parable* is the Greek word "parabole" (pronounced *par-ab-ol-ay*). It translates as "the comparison of one thing with another, a likeness, a similitude, an example by which either the duties of men or the things of God, particularly the nature and history of God's kingdom, are figuratively portrayed." Simply put, "a parable is an earthly story with a heavenly meaning."

The subject of the Kingdom of God is an exhaustive study on which multitudes of books, theses and syllabi have been and will be written. Dr. Kelly Varner (one of my spiritual fathers who has gone home to his reward) stated that many of the books on the Kingdom that that he had read over the years only scratched the surface of the topic's depth. I received the revelation contained in this book as I studied the *kingdom parables* and ministered these truths in my church.

What I have penned in this book didn't come from today's popular teaching on eschatology (the study of end-time events), what I learned in Sunday School as a child, or even what is being taught by many of today's so-called end-time Bible prophecy teachers. It has come from studying these parables in the Greek language, as well as applying them through present-day truth. Some will reject the teachings in this book because of their own misconception with one word: *kingdom*. Those who know me know that I have never shied away from controversial subjects just because the religious world doesn't understand or agree with them.

As an Apostolic leader (of some four plus decades at the re-writing of this book), I have seen daily the condition of the church, where we are, and more importantly, where we need to go! People spend millions of dollars each year on the newest Bible prophecy books, as well as subscribing to end-time gurus' literature predicting the next flood, earthquake, disaster, or even worse, some mathematical or Biblical equation as to the Lord's return.

Some may ask, why do so many televangelists propagate a message absent of hope and restoration of all things—with a doom and gloom eschatological approach?

It's simply - FEAR sells! And even more importantly than the hour of His return (which, by the way which Jesus himself nor the Holy Spirit know), the church should be taught the meaning of Jesus' words. *"Occupy until I come,"* (Luke 19:13). Many of God's people have grown *weary* (Gal. 6:9); some have *"shipwrecked their faith."* (1Tim. 1:19); their *"love has waxed cold."* (Matt. 24:12); or even worse, *"departed from the faith."* (1Tim. 4:1).

Our precious brothers and sisters need to be taught how to live victorious in the HERE AND NOW. They need the great stories of the Bible brought to where they live and applied to their life TODAY. They are asking us how to:

- Live victorious in their marriage.
- Be a light on their job.
- Deal with a rebellious child.
- Handles their finances.
- Walk in peace and joy.
- Be free from fear, discouragement and depression.

They are also asking questions like:

- What am I supposed to do with my life?
- What is my purpose and destiny?
- How do I know when I am in or out of the will of God?
- How do I know if I am called, and if so, to what office or gift?

- How do those parables that Jesus taught relate to me TODAY?

- And if they do, how do I apply their principles?

Much of today's religious circles are still focusing most of their time, attention and effort on the same old song and dance that I have heard since I was old enough to comprehend what was being spoken. They are still discussing and debating what nation some man they call anti-Christ will come from.

Let me remind you of what the Apostle John wrote: *"Little children, it is the last time: and as ye have heard that antichrist shall come, even now are there many antichrists; whereby we know that it is the last time,"* (1 John 2:18).

He stated, *"ye have heard that antichrist* (singular added for emphasis) shall come." He then goes on to reveal that there are many antichrists (plural, added for emphasis) even NOW. The word *antichrist* is two Greek words, *anti* and *Christos* which defines as "anything or anyone that comes against and/or opposes the anointing."

According to John, in his day there were already many manifestations of antichrist. Rather than trying to pin the tail on one person, would we dare even consider the possibility that we have done things that have or would oppose the anointing or the cause of Christ? End-time preachers are still trying to figure out what/who is the Illuminati, will there be literal marks on hands and foreheads or is it some computer chip placed under the skin. They continually declare the end is near (they have been saying that as far back as I can remember) every time some nation rises against another.

They are still professing that there is some large computer in Europe called *The Beast* that will run the world, and finally, they are trying to convince a lethargic church and confused world that God (who is LOVE) is sending all these end-time disasters, killing thousands of people, to teach them a lesson. In my forty-four years of ministry (as of 2019), I have yet to have a single person enter my office for counsel concerned about any of the above statements. Selah!

As we journey together through this book, we will discover how these kingdom parables apply to today's church, individually and corporately. Let's see what we can learn as the scales are removed from our eyes and the religious clutter is removed from our thinking. Get ready to be challenged, changed and blessed!

*Dr. Don D. Hughes*

**Dr. Don D. Hughes**
REV House
Tulsa, OK

# CHAPTER ONE

# THE WHEAT AND THE TARES

O UR FIRST KINGDOM PARABLE is found in Matthew and is commonly referred to as **the wheat and tares** and the story reads: *"Another parable put he forth unto them saying. The kingdom of heaven is likened unto a man which sowed good seed in his field: But while men slept his enemy came and sowed tares among the wheat, and went his way. But when the blade was sprung up, and brought forth fruit, then appeared the tares also. So the servants of the householder came and said unto him, Sir, didst not thou sow good seed in thy field? From whence then hath it tares? He said unto them, An enemy hath done this. The servants said unto him, Wilt thou then that we go and gather them up? But he said, Nay; lest while ye gather up the tares, ye root up also the wheat with them. Let both grow together until the harvest: and in the time of harvest I will say to the reapers, Gather ye together first the tares, and bind them in bundles to burn them: but gather the wheat into my barn."* (13:24-30).

I find it interesting in verse 24 that Jesus uses the word *good* referring to the type of seed sown. Why? If you can sow good seed, you must be able to sow bad seed. The spiritual law of sowing and reaping operates regardless of the type of seed sown.

Remember: even weeds are produced by seeds. Look again at this familiar verse: *"Be not deceived; God is not mocked: for whatsoever a man soweth, that shall he also reap,"* (Gal. 6:7).

In Genesis, chapter 1, we are told that every seed yields (produces) after its own kind. The word *good* in Matthew 13:24 is the Greek word *kalos* (pronounced *kal-os*) which translates as "excellent in its nature and characteristics, therefore well adapted to its end; genuine; approved." We can't expect to get the right results by sowing the wrong seed. This earthly story (parable) has a heavenly (kingdom) message that we must comprehend.

In verse 25 of this parable, it speaks of the enemy coming in and sowing tares while men slept. The word *slept* here is not a reference to closing one's eyes and resting for several hours. It is the Greek word *katheudo* (pronounced *kath-yoo-do)*, defined as "one who yields to slothfulness and sin; one which has become indifferent to their salvation." The reference here is not to a man who slumbers, and then while he can't see, the enemy comes in.

It is describing a man who, over time, maybe even feeling justified (my own emphasis), begins to sow seed (do his own thing) which effects his relationship with God. He becomes slothful (lazy, idle, sluggish, apathetic, inactive) in his relationship with God. He becomes lazy and idle in serving in the house of God. He now is apathetic to the point that he is inactive and makes all the familiar excuses as to why he is the way he is. He is now indifferent to faithful church attendance, giving, and sacrificing for the cause of Christ. The word *enemy* in verse 25 does not initially reference satan, demons, or the like. It is the Greek word *echthros* (pronounced *ech-thros)* and is used in reference to "men who are at enmity with God, those who oppose God in their mind."

It was very revealing to me that verse 24 uses the word *man* in the singular doing the right thing and verse 25 uses the word *men* in the plural doing the wrong thing. Even here I see the remnant concept! It is easy to find more doing wrong and less doing right in most Christian circles. The deception produced is epidemic. Because of the long-suffering of God, (which, by the way, is not eternal) many carry on in their apathy, their luke-warmness and indifference, thinking everything is okay. They even see (with natural vision) something that looks like and appears to be wheat.

However, the word *tares* comes from the Greek word *zizanion* (pronounced *dziz-an-ee-on)*, describing something "resembling wheat (externally), but the grains are black (internally)," Wheat represents salvation and abundance. It is golden in color, which speaks of God's divinity working in and flowing out of His Christ-man. Only at the end of the process is the truth made known. Tares stand straight up (full of pride and self-righteousness) at harvest, almost with a "look who I am and what I have done" attitude. However, wheat is bowed over (full of true humility and worship, thanking the Master for what He has produced in them) at harvest. Look closely again at verse 25; tares are the result of a man who "...went his way." He went his own way, did his own thing, expecting Godly results and blessing. Godly seed produces Godly fruit, and selfish and indifferent sowing produces tares.

The tares mentioned in verse 26 produced from men at enmity with God, didn't even show up until the fruit appeared from good sowing. All things are being made manifest; we will be known by the *fruit produced* (Matt. 7:16). God, I pray that everything hidden be brought to the light *(emphasis mine)!* This may not be popular, but, hear me out [those that have an ear (singular) to hear. . . HEAR (Rev. 2:7, 17)! I believe that all too often we exaggerate the little bit of fruit that can be seen in our own fields (lives) and try to exploit the tares that we find in others. However, we need to remember something that Paul the Apostle wrote to the church at Rome. He revealed that the **wheat and tares** were operating within his own field (life) at the same time. Look again at these verses with that truth in mind:

*"For that which I do I allow not: for what I would, that do I not; but what I hate, that do I. If then I do that which I would not, I consent unto the law that [it is] good. Now then it is no more I that do it, but sin that dwelleth in me. For I know that in me (that is, in my flesh) dwelleth no good thing: for to will is present with me; but how to perform that which is good I find not. For the good that I would I do not: but the evil which I would not, that I do. Now if I do that I would not, it is no more I that do it, but sin that dwelleth in me. I find then a law, that, when I do good, evil is present with me. For I delight in the law of God after the inward man. But I see another law in my members, warring against the law in my mind, and bringing me into captivity to the law of sin which is in my members. O wretched man that I am! Who shall deliver me from the body of this death?"* (Rom. 7:15-24).

Don't forget what he wrote to the Galatian Church! *"For he that soweth to his flesh shall of the flesh reap corruption; but he that soweth to the Spirit shall of the Spirit real life everlasting,"* (Gal. 6:8).

Also, remember this verse written to church in Rome: *For to be carnally minded [is] death; but to be spiritually minded [is] life and peace"* (Rom. 8:6).

The Bible is full of individuals who had wheat and tares working in them at the SAME TIME.

### Old Testament

Adam – God's creation, clothed in glory

Adam – High treason, disobedient

Moses – Spokesman for God, deliverer

Moses – Anger problem, murderer

David – Great king, mighty warrior, worshipper

David – Murderer and adulterer

Elijah – Prophet of God who killed 450 prophets of Baal

Elijah – Full of fear over one woman

Jacob – Deceiver, trickster, supplanter

Israel – Deliverer, one who prevails

Samson – Victorious warrior

Samson – Lust, disobedient to vows

Miriam – Prophetess, psalmist

Miriam – Rebellious against Gods' man

### New Testament

Peter – The revelation of Christ

Peter – Jesus called him satan

Paul – Apostle, church planter, Bible author

Saul – Persecutor and church hater

## Today

Myself – Apostle, pastor, church planter, missionary, author

Myself – Fearful, pornography, selfish

Your name—you know the **wheat** things

Your name—would you be as bold as to fill in this line with the tares?

See my book, *"Will the Spiritual Ones Please Come Forward?"* for an honest, transparent look at my life, my struggles and testimony. In this book, I share my own revealing testimony of being molested as a young boy. That traumatic event opened the door to a tremendous struggle with pornography which literally lasted for years. I was traveling around the world preaching the *truth which sets people free* only to struggle with my own darkness (tare). I would see hundreds born again, filled with the Spirit, healed and delivered in our services each year, only to return to lonely empty hotel rooms and grapple with my own need for deliverance and freedom. I would continually question my own salvation, gifting and calling.

At times, the embarrassment, guilt and shame were more than I could bear. And, the thought of confiding in a preacher to help me in my struggle? What is that saying you always hear in the mobster movies? Forget about it! I had been in far too many ministers' meetings constantly hearing God's spokesmen (ministers) putting down or uncovering another gifts, weaknesses or struggles to make themselves look more spiritual before their peers.

Looking back now over the past four plus decades of ministry, I have seen the trail littered with the fall of many ministers, ones who had shouted judgment the loudest, only to see many fall prey to the very thing they judged in another.

God is raising up and revealing true spiritual fathers in this powerful prophetic day to His people, they are being given an apostolic and prophetic mandate: *"And he shall turn the heart of the fathers to the children, and heart of the children to their fathers, lest I come and smite the earth with a curse,"* (Mal.4:6).

I had wheat and tares both working in me at the same time and seemingly no one to help, let alone explain what was going on in my internals. Listen, there is hope for you to get through this; you will pass the test, and you will get the victory, so don't lose hope. Your latter will be greater than your former. I made it through this process and so will you. Remember, you may have done what they said you did, but you are not who they say you are. Who are *they* anyway? *They* are folks just like you, dealing with the same and/or similar struggles and issues. I trust as you read the rest of this chapter and book that the *"eyes of your understanding will be enlightened,"* (Eph. 1:18).

There are things growing in us at the same time, good and bad. Both are growing together, and in God's timing He will instruct the reapers (you can't be a reaper until you have first sown) to gather together FIRST the tares. By the way, the *sower* and the *reaper* are the same person. . . SELAH!

These words *"gather ye together,"* (Matt. 13:30) are very revealing in the Greek language. It is the word *sullego (pronounced sool-leg-o)*, which comes from two Greek words *sun* and *lego*. These words literally translate as "to collect in order to carry off; to point out with words (God's Word), to speak of, to speak out." In other words, just about the time you would be reaping from what you have sown, the Word of God (*lego*) within you will rise up and speak to the tares, binding them (throwing into chains) from operating (producing) in your life. They will be burned (consumed) by the fire of God in you. This is a kingdom individual walking in their dominion.

*"For our God [is] a consuming fire,"* (Matt. 12:29).

In Mark 7:14-16, Jesus teaches the people what defiles men. Afterward, the disciples were alone with Jesus in the house and asked Him to explain the parable (verse 17). I find the Lord's response to their question rather humorous. Look at verse 18: *"And he saith unto them, Are ye so without understanding also? Do ye not perceive, that whatsoever thing from without entereth into the man, [it] cannot defile him."*

Jesus' answer is quite revealing of His seeming frustration with their inability to understand. *Without understanding* is the Greek word *asunetos* (pronounced *as-oon-aytos*), which translates as "foolish; unintelligent; stupid." In other words, He was saying, what is keeping your mind from perceiving this? You are hearing but NOT hearing. He goes on to say that *out of the heart* (the center of all physical and spiritual life) proceeds what has been planted there. This truth is again revealed in Luke's gospel.

"*A good man out of the good treasure of his heart bringeth forth that which is good; and an evil man out of the evil treasure of his heart bringeth forth that which is evil: for the abundance of the heart his mouth speaketh,*" (Luke 6:45).

What is *sown* in the heart is *reaped*/produced, through the mouth. There is another verse which clearly illustrates this principle: "*Death and life [are] in the power of the tongue: and they that love it shall eat the fruit therof,*" (Prov, 18:21).

*Our language has so much power (authority) that it can cause us to operate in the realm of death or to live apart from sickness, discouragement and fainting, a life that is truly prosperous. We will feed on that which we are intimate with* (Apostle Hughes paraphrase, Prov. 18:21).

Death and life both have power; the power is released through our words. The word *tongue* is also translated as language. Out language spoken is out heart revealed. The word *love* here is the Hebrew word *ahab* (pronounced *aw-hab*) which means "lover; human love for another, for family" and also defined as sexual love. We have choices every day to be intimate with death or life, to produce wheat or tares. Our conversation does reveal what is hidden in our hearts. The Holy Spirit will reveal and remove, only with your permission, the things you don't want to harvest.

As I close out this first chapter, for clarification's sake, I must explain a principle that I believe can be found at times throughout scripture. I believe that in certain instances, verses in the Bible, stories, parables, etc.., can and will have a literal interpretation as well as a spiritual (or prophetic) application. Here is a case in point! That day by the sea, Jesus began teaching the multitudes on the parable of the wheat and tares, in Matthew 13:24-30. The Greek words used in these verses are different than those he used in declared the meaning to His disciples (by their request) later on that evening in the house in verses 36-43.

Example: As Jesus explains the parable to His disciples, He brings to light the literal meaning. He reveals Himself as he man that sowed good seed; the field was the world; the enemy was the devil, etc. He teaches the parable to the multitudes using certain language and Greek words, and then declares the parable to His disciples using different language with different Greek words. I believe that a literal and spiritual application is revealed in this parable.

One thought in closing: Jesus taught a parable referred to as **wheat and tares** earlier that day. The only question produced from the disciples was, *"declare unto us the parable of the tares of the field,"* (verse 36).

Why did they only ask about the tares?

My belief is that they all knew they had them also. I believe you can go a couple of ways with this! 1) Don't get so much tunnel vision with the negative that you fail to realize the positive is also at work. 2) Or, be as concerned about removing tares as you are about revealing (or harvesting) wheat.

Selah!

## Chapter One Reflection

How does this parable speak and/or apply to me?

_____

_____

_____

_____

_____

_____

_____

_____

_____

_____

_____

_____

_____

_____

Action Steps:

What actions should I take today, this week, this month to apply these principles?

_____

_____

_____

_____

_____

_____

_____

_____

_____

_____

_____

_____

_____

Date/Time that these actions were completed?

_____

_____

_____

_____

_____

_____


Closure:

Thoughts, feelings and emotions from these completed actions?

_____

_____

_____

_____

_____

_____

_____

_____

_____

_____

_____

_____

_____

_____

_____

_____

_____

_____

_____

_____

_____

_____

_____

# Chapter Two

# The Mustard Seed

THE SECOND KINGDOM parable that Jesus taught is found in Matthew. We will refer to it as **the mustard seed**. *Another parable put he forth unto them, saying, The kingdom of heaven is like to a grain of mustard seed, which a man took, and sowed in his field: Which indeed is the least of all seeds: but when it is grown, it is the greatest among herbs, and becometh a tree, so that of the birds of the air come and lodge in the branches thereof,"* (13:31-32).

The words **mustard seed** carry some interesting insight from the Greek language. The Greek word *sinapi* (pronounced *sin-ap-ee*) refers to a plant grown in the orient that begins as a single, tiny seed, yet produces a tree, ten feet tall. In Bible numerics, one of the things the number ten (10) represents is "testimony." In other words, no matter what you are facing, no matter what you are going through, if you have sown the incorruptible seed, stand your ground; the harvest of that seed sown will produce a testimony for you and the Kingdom of God.

*"Being born again, not of corruptible seed, but of incorruptible, by the word of God, which liveth and abideth forever,"* (1 Pet. 1:23).

The process of the seed working out its destiny takes time, which is why we are instructed, *"And let us not be weary in well do doing: for in due season well shall reap, if we faint not,"* (Gal. 6:9).

It is also confirmed again in Second Thessalonians 3:13, *"But ye, brethren, be not weary in well doing."*

In the parable, Jesus refers to the mustard seed as the *least of all seeds,* not referring to its importance as much as the actual size (Greek word *micros* translated "little of size"). Don't look at the size of the seed planted, by God's design, the seed will go through several changes of growth until maturity, thus finally seeing the harvest that the seed was designed to produce. That is the awesomeness of God's power; He can take our little that is mixed with faith and produce a great harvest. Remember: He does "exceeding abundantly above…" (See Eph. 3:20).

### The SEED of Obedience Produced a New Level of Ministry

It was the early fall of 2016, as I sat that evening in the living room with my wife, the TV was on, but I was oblivious to what was airing, my wife was playing a game on her tablet unwinding from a busy day in her corporate job. My ministry schedule had been scarce at best, the offerings, well, that was another story. I was extremely discouraged, four plus decades of ministry, I had pioneered and established churches, authored several books as well as ministered in conferences and churches throughout the United States. I had also spoken internationally, trained leaders and national pastors in several parts of Africa, the Philippines, South Korea and Mexico. All for what? Every thought that you can imagine was spinning in my head like an Oklahoma tornado. It seemed at that very moment that the damn broke, the tears began to flow, I buried my head in my hands and said to my wife, "I'm done!"

At that time, I was on Facebook, I had a page but wasn't doing any live teaching or ministry. At best, simply posting a scripture or leadership quote on occasion. I told her as tears streamed down my face, "I'm going on Facebook, social media and letting all my family, friends and ministry acquaintances know that I QUIT." At that moment, I was convinced that my feelings and emotions justified my forthcoming actions. Now, she was crying, saying everything that she thought would possibly encourage me at that vulnerable moment. I made statements to her like, "nobody cares, my ministry friends have forgotten and/or forsaken me, I'm too old, they don't want to hear or receive what's in me after all these years, and I'm finished!" The room went silent which seemed like an eternity.

Several minutes later my cell phone began to ring breaking the silence in the room. I glanced at the screen, it was a minister friend of our family that we had known for over 30 years. I had absolutely no desire to hear from any preacher at that moment but beyond my present emotional state I felt compelled to answer it. I heard the familiar voice of Pastor Steve Vickers from Montgomery, Alabama. "Brother Don, how are you? I've been thinking about you lately." I spouted out the typical, trying to be positive confession stuff because I didn't want him to know I was hurting, frustrated and angry. However, I was lying through my teeth! Why? I didn't want to be judged for saying the wrong things, I didn't want to be judged for *not* being in faith! Let me just state right here that being honest and transparent is in no way an indictment against your faith. It can be a revealing and acknowledging that begins the process of healing and restoration. It can lead to an awakening that causes you to put your hand back on the plow and once again move forward advancing His kingdom through obedience to your call and fulfilling your purpose.

After a few minutes of basic surface conversation, Pastor Steve began the purpose of his God's perfect timing call. "Don, let me ask you a question, doesn't Romans 11:29 say that the gifts and calling of God are without repentance?" I immediately responded, "Yes sir, it does." He continued, "God called you and placed His gifts in you even before you came through your mother's womb (see Jer. 1:5). He knew every situation that you would go though, every decision that you would make, right and wrong, and knowing all of this He still called you. I know that He is not finished with you because you are still breathing. I want you to promise me something." At this point he had my undivided attention based on the timing of the call and the subject of our conversation. "What do you want me to do sir?" He continued by encouraging me in my gift and calling and then stated the following. "Don, go on Facebook regularly, weekly, teach from your books, share your heart, tell your story, and be real and transparent. That's really what people want and need to hear." In honor to him and the long relationship he had with our family, I agreed.

That first week, I did my first live teaching, I spoke less than five minutes and finished. To be completely transparent, my thoughts were, "ok, I kept my promise, I did the live" and then those familiar with Facebook will understand the following. My phone made a beep on my Facebook app that someone had PM'd (Private messaged) me. I clicked on the man's message and it was a minister who thanked me for my honesty and encouragement. The very first live!

Over two years have passed (at the re-writing of this manuscript) since that first Facebook live, now my weekly teachings, tag-team ministry and interviews are seen by thousands every week around the world. New ministry doors are continually opening, more than 80% of our ministry schedule are new contacts developed through the venue of Social Media. Before I launched that first live teaching, I didn't' have three meetings scheduled over a three-month period. Now I average three plus meetings every month throughout the US, Canada, and abroad. BUT GOD! Thank you, Pastor Steve, from the bottom of my heart for your obedience, your love and your belief in my purpose and gift. One final thought in closing, recently I received an update from Facebook (I'm not sure how all that information is kept) at the re-writing and updating of this manuscript congratulating me on over 150,000 views of my videos. Right then I realized how many people have been encouraged, challenged, impacted and even changed through my obedience.

Receive this prophetic encouragement. There is much Kingdom work yet to be done, He wasn't finished with me and neither is He with you. Get back up, stand back up, shake off the dust, refocus, refuel. Your best is NOT behind you, it's in FRONT of you. Clock back in, put your hand back on the plow. The Glory of the latter is greater. I promise!

At the updating of this book (January 2019), I once again find myself in transition as to the next season of ministry. In January 2019, myself, along with my friend, Dr. Barry Cook, will be releasing a radical, relevant, and raw TV series called *God's Garage* tackling real issues with real talk. We are also launching a new ministry plant in Tulsa, Oklahoma in May of 2019. It will be team led emphasizing the development of 5-fold ministry, restoring people and raising up leaders for this new day.

God is always faithful, and the seed of His purpose, destiny, and calling still burns inside of me as I believe it does you. My best days are yet to come and so are yours. Don't look at the size of the seed; but look at what that seed can produce when planted!

Let's return to the parable.

In this parable of the Mustard Seed, verse 32 uses the word *grown* which carries the idea of internal increase and growth, growing from the inside-out. This is why so many judge people and things prematurely, because the seed is working from the inside-out. It is working when you don't necessarily feel anything. It is working in the unseen realm, moving towards the seen or revealed realm. The seeds process begins in the INTERNALS.

Again, that is why the Apostle Paul wrote this statement to the Church at Corinth: *"Therefore judge nothing before the time, until the Lord come, who both will bring to light the hidden things of darkness, and will make manifest the counsels of the hearts: and then shall every man have praise of God,"* (1 Cor. 4:5).

All of us move through seasons in our lives, both naturally and spiritually. However, hardly ever are we in them together at the same time. Just some food for thought: Basically, there are four seasons we experience each year (winter, spring, summer, and fall); each season lasts approximately 90 days. The number 9 represents gifts and fruit, but it also deals with birth. Each season, if allowed to work as it is designed to, will bring us to more growth and maturity in our lives individually, and ultimately, corporately.

Spring = Planting,

Summer = Growing and Developing,
Fall = Harvest,
Winter = Pruning and Barrenness

This is a time of preparation...NOT punishment! Don't lose heart! You are 90 days away from a new season. Verse 32 references the progression of the seed. The seed is planted, grows, becomes great and ultimately becomes a tree. The word tree is the Greek word *dendron* (pronounced *dendron*), which describes an oak. It also comes from another Greek word, *agape*, which translates as love. It is a reference to the highest form of love there is; it literally the LOVE OF GOD. Using the Greek word *agape* here is extremely important.

The love walk is vital in order for the seed planted to become a full-grown (mature) tree. Remember: It was God's unconditional love that planted the greatest seed (His Son) into the earth. That seed died, was buried, and rose again. The seed (Christ) fulfilled its/His destiny. The absence of the love of God in our lives can hinder or stunt our growth, dwarfing our potential, possibly even causing us to miss our God-given destiny.

Speaking truth and walking in truth causes growth when it is done *in love*. Do you remember what the Apostle Paul wrote to the church at Ephesus? *"But speaking the truth in love, may we grow up into him in all things, which is the head [even] Christ,"* (Eph. 4:15).

In this kingdom parable, the word **mustard** carries some interesting thought. Herbert Lockyer, in his book *All the Parables of the Bible,* states that the word mustard is the Arabic word "khardah" which symbolizes small beginnings, ever so little, the smallest weight or measure. Because of the seed's hot, fiery vigor, and giving only its best virtues when BRUISED, it is therefore attractive to the taste of birds who are drawn to the herb for food and shelter" (used by permission).

Look again at the statement *birds of the air* in Matthew 13:32. Did you notice when the birds show up? They show up when the seed becomes a tree! At this point, the tree has the potential to produce *fruit*. Birds of the air often symbolize satan and subtle forces. For example, Matthew identifies the birds of the air as the *wicked one*. Mark speaks of them as symbolizing *satanic activity*. Luke links the fowls of the air to the *devil*.

I find Herbert Lockyer's use of the word *bruise* in explaining the Arabic word for *mustard* eye-opening revealing great prophetic insight. The **mustard seed** is the fruit of the *mustard tree*. The bird (enemy) is not so much after the fruit of the *mustard tree*. The bird (enemy) is not so much after the fruit in our lives as much as what the fruit can produce.

It is when we are being crushed, bruised, and pressured that the Christ-like virtues that are inside of us begin to manifest, especially to a world that desperately needs to see the true CHRIST. The bird (enemy) doesn't show up because there is sin in our lives; it shows up because fruit is being manifested that not only affects us; but can and will impact the lives of those around us.

Let's consider another passage of scripture referring to these birds. In Genesis, chapter 15, beginning in verse 1, God reveals Himself to Abram in a vision. He begins to speak to Abram's destiny. Abram stops Him (as we so often do) and begins to make excuses.

Then Abram's statement in verse 3 caught my attention: *"And Abram said, Behold, to me thou has given no seed: and, lo, one born in my house is mine heir,"* (Gen. 15:3).

Abram knew that seed was needed to bring the *Word of the Lord* to pass that had been prophesied over him. God shows him the heavens and the stars as a prophetic gesture (a sign), revealing the potential that seed could produce if allowed to run its course. God asked Abram if he could count the stars, and of course, the answer was no. All too often, we expend too much time and far too much energy gazing at the size of the seed instead of focusing our faith on the seed's potential.

Abram begins to sacrifice to the Lord over what God declared concerning his future (Gen. 15:7, 13-14, 18-21). On more than one occasion, the scriptures reveals praise as a sacrifice: *"By him therefore let us offer the sacrifices of praise to God continually, that is, the fruit of [our] lips giving thanks to his name,"* (Heb. 13:15). Men lift themselves to a higher place as they bring a praise sacrifice, totally surrendered, honoring and extolling God with their mouth wide open, acknowledging Him as God Almighty. (Apostle Hughes paraphrase)

*"And it shall be, [that] whoso will not come up of [all] the families of the earth unto Jerusalem o worship the King, the LORD of hosts, even upon them shall be no rain,"* (Zech. 14:17). Praise and worship bring rain (spiritually), which causes the planted seed to grow, the mathematical equation is simple:

No worship = No rain= No growth.

Many ultra-Pentecostal's, (my terminology) praise, worship and shout after the manifestation. Kingdom people praise before conception; they praise during the growth and transition of the seed, as well as at the end, which is the maturity of the seed (the promise).

Here is a final thought in closing out this parable: The word fowls in Genesis 15:11 is a different Hebrew word than the word birds in verse 10. The word fowls is the Hebrew work *"ayit"* (pronounced *ah-yit)* which describes a bird of prey, a ravenous (greedy) bird. If praise helps grow the seed (and it does), the bird's (enemy's) plan is to hinder our sacrifice, thus thwarting the seeds potential, it's destiny. GET YOUR PRAISE ON! The SEED has a designated driver. It's you in "P" for praise, not "P" for park.

## Chapter Two Reflections

How does this parable speak and/or apply to me?

_____

_____

_____

_____

_____

_____

_____

_____

_____

_____

_____

Actions Steps:

What actions should I take today, this week, this month to apply these principles?

_____

_____

_____

_____

_____

_____

_____

_____

_____

_____

_____

_____

_____

Date/Time that these actions were completed?

_____

_____

_____

_____

_____

_____

_____

_____

_____

Closure:

Thoughts, feelings and emotions from these completed actions?

_____

_____

_____

_____

_____

_____

_____

_____

_____

_____

_____

_____

_____

_____

_____

_____

_____

# CHAPTER THREE

# THE LEAVEN

THE THIRD KINGDOM parable that Jesus taught is found in Matthew. It is the parable of **the leaven**. We will refer to it as **the mustard seed**. *"Another parable spake he unto them; the kingdom of heaven is like unto leaven, which a woman took, and hid in three measures of meal, till the whole was leavened. All these things spake Jesus unto he multitude in parables; and without a parable spake he not unto them; that it might be fulfilled which was spoken by the prophet, saying, I will open my mouth in parables; I will utter things which have been kept secret from the foundation of the world,"* (13:33-35).

In many instances, the word **leaven** has a negative connotation and is often used in a bad sense. However, here in this parable it is used in the positive. The word *leaven* is the Greek word *"ezum"* (pronounced *dzoo-may*). It is viewed in its tendency to INFECT others. Leaven is applied to that which, though small in quantity, yet by its influence thoroughly saturates and infuses a thing (#2219 Thayer's). The word *leaven* also comes from another Greek word *"zeo"* (pronounced *dzeb-o*), which translates "to be fervent; hot; boiling over with love and zeal for what is GOOD" (#2204 Thayer's).

During the days of Jesus' earthly ministry, they would take a piece of leavened dough from an unbaked loaf and put it among the new dough to cause fermentation (I will deal with this a little later in the chapter). I see the woman in this parable as a prophetic look at the church. Many believe the ekklesia (church) to be the bride of Christ, thus referencing the church in the feminine gender (and remember that the church is the instrument used in revealing God's Kingdom). In Matthew 13:3, the verse states this woman took the leaven. The word took is the Greek word *"lambano"* (pronounced *lam-*

*ban-o*), which describes a person "receiving or taking hold of." The male (Christ) releases the seed (1 Pet. 1:23), and the woman (the church), receives the seed. Don't forget that this whole thing began with a prophecy from God Himself that a seed was coming. (See Genesis 3:15).

Who is the seed?

*"Now to Abraham and his seed were the promises made. He saith not, And to the seeds, as of many; but as of one, And to thy seed, which is Christ,"* (Gal. 3:16).

Where is the seed?

*"To whom God would **make known** what [is] the riches of the glory of his **mystery** among the Gentiles; which is Christ in you the hope of glory,"* (Col. 1:27, bold added for emphasis).

This leaven (that which by its influence thoroughly saturates and infuses a thing) has been hidden, waiting to be revealed. The word hid is the Greek word *"ekgrupto"* (pronounced *eng-kroop-to*), which translates as "something that has been concealed; to mingle one thing with another." The church may not look or even feel pregnant, but be assured of one thing: SHE IS, and the thing she is carrying is HOLY, and it will look like the FATHER. The church has carried this hidden thing through two (2) of the Lord's days and has now entered into the beginning, at least the first fruits of the 3rd day.

Remember what Peter wrote in the epistles: *"But, beloved, be not ignorant of this one thing, that one day [is] with the Lord as a thousand years, and a thousand years as one day,"* (2 Pet. 3:8).

From Adam to Christ was four (4) days, or four thousand (4000) years, and from Christ to today is three (3) days, or three thousand (3000) years. This woman (the church) received the seed that has been *concealed* in the past, waiting to be *revealed* in the NOW. The term *three measures of meal* can also describe three different *periods* of measure. The seed has come through **justification**, moved on into **sanctification**, and now into GLORIFICATON. It has come through the outer court, on into the holy place, and now going beyond the veil into the holy of holies. We have seen and experienced different measures (seasons) of anointing; however, this is the time for the GLORY. Haggai 2:9 states, *"The glory of this latter house shall be* *greater than of the former, saith the LORD of hosts; and in this place I will give peace, saith the LORD of hosts."*

The Apostle Paul inscribed these words to the Corinthian church: *"For we know in part, and we prophesy in part. 10 But when that which is perfect is come, then that which is in part shall be done away,"* (1 Cor. 13:9-10).

Much of what we have taught and prophesied has been in parts or pieces; yet, this is the season that all the pieces are coming together. The hidden seed in the church has been growing, even thru great persecution and affliction. We are in our 3ʳᵈ trimester; we are walking funny (the thing we are carrying is bigger that we are); we have been emotional and irritable, difficult to live with or even be around. If I can so bold, there is always pleasure in receiving the seed; it is only after the seed has been planted that all the pain, transition and difficulty begin to manifest. That is when many begin to question what has happened and make statements like "What is going on IN me? Is all this really going to be worth it? I don't like this! You did this to me! Then the statement, my clothes don't fit. No, of course they don't, this new revelation (seed) is bigger than what your old clothes could handle, and the old wine skins don't fit this new release of wine, thus the new outfits to handle the new growth. SELAH!

What is coming up and out in this measure (season, period) is the seed fully developed, matured (complete). The fruit of the seed (Christ) that had been hidden is being revealed, the seed's true DNA is being made manifest. Christ IN US, the revealing of HIS GLORY. We are no longer speaking in rhymes or riddles, prophesying in part, or even teaching in part. We are revealing the WHOLE counsel of God to those who have an ear to hear.

The Apostle Paul further states in verse 12: *"For now we see through a glass, darkly; but then face to face: now I know in part; but then shall I know even as also I am known,"* (1 Cor. 13:12).

He also wrote to the church in Rome and declared: *"Now to him that is of power to stablish you according to my gospel, and the preaching of Jesus Christ, according to the revelation of the mystery, which was kept secret since the world begin, But now is made manifest, and by the scriptures of the prophets, according to the commandment of the everlasting God, made known all nations for the obedience of faith,"* (Rom. 16:25-26).

He said the revelation of the mystery had been kept secret, the Greek word for *secret* is *"sigao"* (pronounced *see-gah-o*) speaks of something *being kept in silence or concealed.* Let me insert something here that I see as very significant. God gave Moses the pattern of the tabernacle in the wilderness and told him to build it (Exodus). He gave the pattern from the inside-out (the holy of holies to the outer court). He started with the holy of holies (the hidden secret place) and worked His way OUT. You work OUT your own salvation from the inside out, and ultimately what's been hidden IN YOU will be revealed in the SEEN REALM for all to see.

*"Wherefore, my beloved, as ye have always obeyed, not as in my presence only, but now much more in absence, work out your own salvation with fear and trembling."* (Phil. 2:12).

In religion, people always look at, judge and only want to deal with what is external, what is visible, what can be seen. Don't forget: Man looks on the outward appearance, but God looks on the heart. *"But the LORD said unto Samuel, Look not on his countenance, or on the height of his stature; because I have refused him: for {the LORD seeth} not as man seeth; for man looketh on the outward appearance, but the LORD looketh on the heart,"* (1 Sam. 16:7).

For a moment, let's return to Christianity 101. You are spirit (Holy of Holies), you have a soul (holy place), and you live in a body (outer court). God brings revelation to your spirit; then that truth works its way through your mind, will and emotions, then your renewed mind gets in agreement with your spirit and finally lived out through your life.

Look at First Corinthians 2:10-12: *"But God hath revealed [them] unto us by his Spirit: for the Spirit searcheth all things, yea, the deep things of God. For what man knoweth the things of a man, save the spirit of man which is in him? Even so he things of God knoweth no man, but the Spirit of God. Now we have received, not the spirit of the world, but the spirit which is of God; that we might know the things that are freely given to us of God."*

Revelation and truth are revealed to your spirit, transferred to and through the soul (mind, will, and emotions), and then seen and lived out through your body (the image of God). Remember: We have been given the mind of Christ (the ability to think like Christ). *"But we have the mind of Christ,"* (1 Cor. 2:16).

A final thought in closing this parable: The woman (church) received the seed, and it remained hidden while growing and developing through different measure (periods, seasons). The sign of her readiness is that the WHOLE was leavened (infected, influenced). Christ's many-membered body must become whole, complete and entire. Everyone in God's kingdom fits somewhere in the overall picture! Every joint supplieth! The message of the Kingdom has been hid and is now being revealed in truth, demonstration, and power.

In the natural, one of the signs that we are growing up is that our vocabulary, communication and language become more developed. I believe that principle applies to us spiritually, as well. Our language should be increasing and expanding as we grow up IN HIM in all things (Eph. 4:15). There is a season where it is ok to talk baby talk, then your language increases as you move in and through the infant, toddler, child, adolescent, youth and finally the adult stages. The early stages of communication in the infant, toddler, child, adolescent and youth stages are always wrapped around them, what they need. Example: I need fed, I need changed, I need held, I need attention, I need played with (I think you get the picture). As we grow into adulthood it becomes about others.

Remember Jesus' words in the garden *"not my will but thine be done"* (Luke 22:42). There is a language in God's kingdom that is being declared; are we grown up enough that we can understand, perceive, and communicate it? It has been in us all along waited to be developed then delivered. We must all move away from thinking, speaking and understanding like a child, it is time to put those things away from us and BE THE MAN and WOMAN God purposed from the beginning of time (1 Cor. 13:11).

## Chapter Three Reflections

How does this parable speak and/or apply to me?

_____

_____

_____

_____

_____

_____

_____

_____

_____

_____

_____

_____

_____

_____

_____

_____

Action Steps:

What actions should I take today, this week, this month to apply these principles?

_____

_____

_____

_____

_____

_____

_____

_____

Date/Time that these actions were completed?

_____

_____

_____

_____

_____

_____

_____

_____

_____

_____

Closure:

Thoughts, feelings and emotions from these completed actions?

_____

_____

_____

_____

_____

_____

_____

_____

_____

_____

_____

_____

_____

_____

_____

_____

_____

_____

# Chapter Four

# The Hidden Treasure

THE FOURTH KINGDOM parable that Jesus taught is found in Matthew's gospel. It is the parable of **the hidden treasure**. *"Again, the kingdom of heaven is like unto treasure hid in a field; he which when a man hath found, he hideth and for joy thereof goeth and selleth all that he hath, and buyeth the field,"* (13:44).

I find it worthy to note that in the first few parables (chapters) which we have covered, much of the information revealed in Jesus' teaching deals with things that are *planted* (hidden), *processed* (the procedure of progression), and ultimately *produced* (made manifest). Again, for repetition's sake (stating It enough until one gets it), look at how the church has digressed concerning judging things/people prematurely or externally.

Once more, pay close attention to the truth discovered in this verse: *"Therefore judge nothing before the time, until the Lord come, who both will bring to light the hidden things of darkness, and will make manifest the counsels of the hearts: and shall every man have praise of God,"* (1 Cor. 4:5).

There is a cycle (a process) the seed MUST experience to reach its destiny. The seed is planted, then dies, and then comes the blade, the ear, the full corn, and finally, it is harvested (John 12:24; Mark 4:28-29).

*"Verily, verily, I say unto you, Except a corn of wheat fall into the ground and die, it abideth alone: but if it die, it bringeth forth much fruit,"* (John 12:24)

*"For the earth bringeth forth fruit of herself; first the blade, then the ear, after that the full corn in the ear. But when the fruit if brought forth,*

*immediately he putteth in the sickle, because the harvest is come,"* (Mark 4:28-29)

The "hid treasure" kingdom parable has tremendous *present truth* application. The thesaurus uses many words for "treasure," like *money, riches, wealth, fortune, jewels, gold, silver, cache, hoard, booty, and plunder.* In this parable. The word "treasure" comes from the Greek word *"thesauros"* (pronounced *thay-sow-ros*), characterized as "the place in which precious and goods things are collected and laid up." The Apostle Paul said it this way:

*"But we have this treasure in earthen vessels, that the excellency of the power may be of God, and not of us,"* (2 Cor. 4:7).

Your physical body comes from the earth; thus, Paul refers to you as an "earthen vessel." *"And the LORD God formed man [of] the dust of the ground and breathed into his nostrils the breath of life; and man became a living soul,"* (Gen. 2:7).

Our Western civilization entrusts its valuables, riches, etc. to banks for safe keeping; yet, in ancient Eastern civilizations, they would (and some still do) bury their valuables in fields or gardens to save them from robbers or potential accidents. God has already planted our spiritual DNA in each of us. It has been concealed in our earth, waiting for the "set time" to be revealed. Why did Jesus buy back (redeem, ransom) the field (world) with His life? To harvest what God had already planted in it/you. Re-read Genesis, chapter 1: some of the things God put into/on the earth were *created*, but some were in *seed form*, yet to be revealed.

In the gospels, there are several references to treasure being in the heart of man (unseen realm, internals). Every one of us has God-given seed planted in our hearts relating to our calling and destiny. Decisions, choices, actions, seasons, relationships, people, etc. either move our seed to maturity (growth and development), or the negative side of wrong decisions, choices, actions, seasons, relationships, people, etc., will hinder the seed from growing and producing. Wrong decisions have been the death sentence to many destinies of God's people, thus never seeing the seed produce the treasure God had planted in them. We must get around people who "plant and water." Another thought: spend time with those who *celebrate* you, not with those who *tolerate* you.

*"I have planted, Apollos watered; but God gave the increase,"* (1 Cor. 3:6).

Stay away from those who tear down or try to uproot what God is building/has planted in you.

For example: It was amazing to me the comments that I begin to hear from ministers (black and white) when I began to reveal the seed God had spoken to me concerning the raising up of a multicultural ministry in Charlotte, North Carolina in late 1999 (what many refer to as the Deep South). Statements like, "This is the South. It is still too segregated. You won't be able to get black and white folks to come to the same church, there are far too many differences and issues." These ministers definitely were NOT watering the seed that God had planted in my spirit. They were unknowingly trying to uproot the seed that burned within my heart. Just because it hasn't happened for them or with others doesn't mean it won't happen with you! Be careful who you reveal your seed to; they may be unknowingly prophesying with their words and actions a crop failure.

Let's look again at Matthew 13:44. This parable uses the word "joy" in reference to the realization/revelation that something awesome that had been hidden, was *yet to be revealed*. The word *joy* is the Greek word *"chara"* (pronounced *khar-ah*), which describes a cause or occasion of great joy or gladness.

These are a few things that can be applied here:

- Understand the lengths God went to in planting His plan and purpose into your life.
- Understand how much He loves you and chooses to believe the best – NO MATTER WHAT IS SEEN AT PRESENT.
- Understand the GREAT JOY that Father receives from those whose life becomes the very thing He planned for it to be.

The other side of the coin is this: When you realize the awesomeness of God's plan for your life and the potential the seed has in it, you should be full of joy during the entire process knowing and being reminded of promises like: *"Being confident of this very thing, that he which hath begun a good work in you will perform [it] until the day of Jesus Christ,"* (Phil. 1:6).

*"The LORD will perfect [that which] concerneth me: thy mercy, O LORD, [endureth] forever: forsake no the works of thine own hands,'* (Ps. 138:8).

Don't forget, God is continually "watching over His word" (seed) to perform it (Jer. 1:12). When you understand how valuable the message is that God has planted inside of you, you will go through what you have to go through, give or give up what you have to, go where He says go, and do whatever it takes for His Kingdom to be revealed IN and THROUGH you. The Kingdom of God is within you (Luke 17:21); the time of revealing is NOW. You were designed to have more than leaves; you are not a fruitless tree, and the seed of greatness in IN you. You have been created and called to bring forth FRUIT, and that fruit is to REMAIN.

*"Ye have not chosen me, but I have chosen you, and ordained you, that ye should go and bring forth fruit, and [that] our fruit should remain: that whatsoever ye shall ask of the Father in my name, he may give it you,"* (John 15:16).

The greatest thing NOW being revealed is the CHRIST. The Layers of religious mindsets and man-made traditions are being detached; all things that have blurred and even distorted HIS TRUE IMAGE are being stripped away. Christ has been sermonized through so many layers of men's doctrine that the truth has been difficult to see. The Apostle Paul uncovered truth in his writings to the Colossian church that had been concealed from people (generations) and periods of time (ages). What has been "hid" is NOW being revealed.

Look at these verses in *Colossians: [Even] the mystery which hath been hid from ages and from generations, but now is made manifest to his saints: to whom God would make known what [is] the riches of the glory of this mystery among the Gentiles; which is Christ in you, the hope of glory,"* (1:26-27).

God was preparing for intimacy again. The first time was with His creation man (Gen. 1:27). This next time would be with His NEW creation man:

*"Therefore if any man [be] in Christ, [he is] a new creature: old things are passed away; behold, all things are become new,"* (2 Cor. 5:17).

"All that is in the Messiah is therefore The New Creation; the old order has passed away to such," (2 Cor. 5:17, Aramaic Bible in Plain English)

Whoever is a believer in Christ is a new creation; the old way of living has disappeared.  A new way of living has come into existence. (God's Word Translation)

When you accepted Christ, the seeds of past failures, seeds of wrong choices and seeds of spiritual bankruptcy were passed away; the Greek word "parerchomai" (pronounced *par-er-khom-ahee*), denotes *something perishing, never making a public appearance* (definition from Thayer's #3928 and #2064). The King James Version finishes verse 17 "...all things are become new." The original language says that "something new, recently made, fresh, unprecedented and uncommon is coming into existence, coming center stage, being made public before men."

What is happening? The mystery (the hidden purpose and counsel) of God is NOW BEING MADE MANIFEST, which is CHRIST IN YOU, the assurance of the GLORY being revealed in and through His body (you and me) in this 3rd day (See my book, *The 3rd Day, The Spirit of Revelation*).

## Chapter Four Reflections

How does this parable speak and/or apply to me?

_____

_____

_____

_____

_____

_____

_____

_____

_____

_____

Actions Steps:

What actions should I take today, this week, this month to apply these principles?

_____

_____

_____

_____

_____

_____

_____

_____

_____

_____

_____

_____

Date/Time that these actions were completed?

_____
_____
_____
_____
_____
_____
_____
_____

Closure:

Thoughts, feelings and emotions from these completed actions:

_____
_____
_____
_____
_____
_____
_____
_____
_____
_____
_____
_____
_____
_____
_____
_____
_____
_____
_____
_____

# Chapter Five

# The Pearl

THE NEXT KINGDOM parable, being only two verses long, reveals incredible insight into present-day truth: *"Again the kingdom of heaven is like unto a merchant man, seeking goodly pearls: who, when he had found one pearl of great price, went and sold all that he had, and bought it,"* (Matt. 13:45-46).

Remember: A parable is an *earthly story* with a *heavenly meaning*. This "merchant man" is a reference to an individual on a journey. Many describe their life as a journey, and the Bible also refers to it as a race.

*"Know ye not that they which run in a race run all, but one receiveth the prize? So run, that ye may obtain,"* (1Cor. 9:24).

*"Wherefore seeing we also are compassed about with so great a cloud of witnesses, let us lay aside every weight, and the sin which doth so easily beset [us],"* (Heb. 12:1).

The Greek word for *pearl* is *"margarites"* (pronounced *mar-gar-ee-tace*), which in its simplest form defines as a pearl oyster. This word also translates as a "proverb, a word of great value." As people in God's Kingdom, our lives should be moving from faith to faith: *"For therein is the righteousness of God revealed from faith to faith: as it is written, the just shall live by faith,"* (Rom. 1:17).

We are also moving from glory to glory: *"But we all, with open face beholding as in a glass the glory of the Lord, are changed into the same image from glory to glory, [even] as by the Spirit of the Lord,"* (2 Cor. 3:18).

In this process called life, we will need to hear, receive, and act continually upon "words of great value" (proverbs). It is the *application* of these proverbs that bring us the victory.

*"But be ye doers of the word, and not hearers only, deceiving your own selves. For if any be a hearer of the word, and not a doer, he is like unto a man beholding his natural face in a glass: For he beholdeth himself, and goeth his way, and straightway forgetteth what manner of a man he was. But whoso looketh into the perfect law of liberty, and continueth [therein], he is being not a forgetful hearer, but a doer of the work, this man shall be blessed in his deed,"* (James 1:22-25).

James 1:22-25 reminds us that "doers of the word" are blessed. Since these pearls are needed and produced along life's journey, let's examine some awesome prophetic insight into the development and purpose. Many think that natural pearls start their development with a grain of sand. Pearl oysters live on the bottom of the ocean's floor where they can get all the sand they want. Actually, a pearl oyster is capable of getting rid of sand, bits and pieces of shell or coral, as well as little pebbles.

The true reason behind the natural formation of a pearl comes from a parasite, an actual drilling worm that literally drills through the shell of the pearl oyster. As this foreign matter begins to work its way into the life of the oyster, the oyster becomes irritated and uses its only method of defense to form a barrier. This defense is actually called a MANTLE.

This mantle is an organ that produces the oyster's shell. The mantle uses the minerals from the oyster's food to produce its COVERING. (Oh, I trust that you are seeing the spiritual truths here). The material produced by the mantle is called *"nacre"* (pronounced *na-ker*), which begins to line the INSIDE of the oyster's shell. This *anointing (my word used for emphasis)* starts overcoming the intruder with layer upon layer of the nacre until it turns *tragedy into triumph, a mess into a message, a test into a testimony, finally producing a pearl of great price.*

The secretion produced by the mantle is a pearly substance known as the "mother of pearl." Many of these precious pearls during their process grow to approximately 8mm and become very valuable. The biblical meaning for the number eight (8) is a number that represents a *new beginning.* What the enemy thought would be the end of you is just the beginning of something new, wonderful, and extremely valuable.

*What the enemy meant for bad . . .*

The call no parent ever wants to hear came on a very hot late spring afternoon in Scottsdale, Arizona as I was out walking through model homes and dreaming of owning my own one day. My friend, Prophet Wynn Hinson, who was staying in my home at that time called, and the call went like this: "Don, you need to come home right away. Aaron [my youngest son] has been in an automobile accident, and they've *life-lined* him to a local hospital in Tulsa, Oklahoma."

There was silence on both ends of the phone that seemed like an eternity. Over the next few hours, calls were made, airline tickets purchased, and I was on a plane headed to Tulsa. I was going there with one thought in mind, *If Aaron passed before I got there, I would raise him up.* After all, God had used myself and others once before to raise up a man who had died in a restaurant in Florida. Every thought and emotion that you could imagine was twirling around my mind like an F-5 tornado. I cried, encouraged myself in the Lord (as the Psalmist David did) during the flight, spoke the promises of God... I did everything I knew and was taught to do.

My father picked me up at the airport, and we drove straight to the hospital. I nodded at family and friends in the waiting room and walked straight to the room where they had Aaron. You are never really prepared to see your baby boy (then sixteen years old and just over 6' tall) hooked up to every machine imaginable, tubes running in and out of him, etc. At that point, they were basically keeping him alive. Our family and friends prayed (in English and in the Spirit), prophesied, spoke the Word...We did everything we knew to do and had taught others to do for years.

At one point, shortly after midnight, as I stood at his bed, alone in the room, I cried out to the Lord and I remember saying to Him, "If you have ever spoke to me in my life and ministry, I need you to speak to me now." After what seemed like forever, I heard these words so strong in my spirit: "He isn't coming back. I gave him a choice." Let me just say right here, in all my years of ministry, all the interviews that I have seen with those who have shared "death to life" and "out of body experiences" and the things they have described, I had to come to terms within myself concerning my perception of eternity. With the Lord giving my son a choice, and him choosing "eternity" over coming back to earth, family and friends, I'm not convinced that we truthfully don't have much insight/revelation about eternity.

Over the next several hours, many decisions were made, with the final one being that we would release his organs to help save others' lives, and that his body would be used for medical science. His final remains would be cremated and given to the family.

If I may be completely transparent right here, it is easy to preach and prophesy what we say we believe until "what we believe" is tested. The loss of my youngest son was the greatest attack against my ministry and calling that I had ever faced up to that point in my life. It was an all-out attack to ultimately get me out of ministry altogether, to challenge my beliefs and what I taught. What the enemy thought would be the end of my ministry didn't quite work as planned. Walking out of the hospital early the next morning after saying my final goodbye to Aaron, I made him a promise. I promised him that his death would not be in vain and that I would not quit. I promised him that I would preach, prophesy, and do all that God desired of me.

Since that promise, I am in the process on my second church plant (This one in Tulsa, Oklahoma, late spring of 2019), I have authored five books and am working on my sixth, I have ministered in seven different countries. I have given apostolic oversight and counsel to ministers, leaders and churches in the United States, as well as abroad.

I have restored prodigal sons and daughters in the US, as well as other regions around the world. I have become a "Nehemiah" type of ministry, rebuilding walls of trust among the races. We raised up sons and daughters with an apostolic and prophetic mandate to IMPACT their city, region, nation, and world with the message of The Kingdom, 5-fold Team Ministry and Corporate Anointing. I am humbled by all of this and give God ALL the glory. What the enemy thought would cause me to throw in the towel, actually released a NEW beginning, commitment and consecration.

As we go further into this parable, I want to share a truth found in Isaiah 59:19 that many don't realize. In the original language, there are no chapter divisions, no lower case letters, no punctuation or division by verse. The translators did this to help make the Bible read better.

In the King James Version of the Bible, part of verse 19 reads: *"When the enemy shall come in like a flood, the Spirit of the LORD shall lift up a standard against him."*

As it reads this way, it makes the enemy the powerful flood. However, when I move the comma over three words, look how the emphasis changes:

*"When the enemy shall come in, LIKE A FLOOD the Spirit of the LORD shall lift up a standard against him,"* (comma moved; caps added for emphasis).

When the intruder (parasite) is attempting to come in to bring destruction, the anointing floods the compartments of your life with the nacre that turns his plan for pain and destruction into a pearl (one that has cost a great price to produce). It becomes a proverb, a story with a happy, victorious ending. Don't get caught up in despair, discouragement, or fear when the beginning of a thing seems disastrous; you're latter WILL BE GREATER than your former. We have that promise.

Look at this statement in Ecclesiastes 7:8: *"Better [is] the end of a thing than the beginning thereof..."*

"I prophesy right now under the unction of the Holy Spirit, that every intruder, every irritant that has found a foothold, a place of entry into your life, shall be overcome by the anointing, the nacre within. Every weapon that has been or is being formed against you, it will not be for your destruction; but will produce a pearl of great price. The attacks against your spirit, soul, and body will be thwarted by the mantle of God upon and in your life, and words of great value, proverbs of victory, are forthcoming that will impact the lives of multitudes. What the enemy has meant for your destruction will only produce pearls of tremendous value in the Kingdom of God. Keep your hand to the plow; keep His purpose top priority in your life. You're coming out more valuable that before the attack started."

As a friend of mine always says and has written, "It's ALL GOOD!" Let me paraphrase a couple of the verses of scripture as we close out this chapter.

"I see clearly now; my perception and discernment are accurate. No matter what I'm facing, I will keep my constitution upright and honorable, continually walking in God's love because my vocation is set; it's ALL good. I will come out on top," (Rom. 8:28, Apostle Hughes paraphrase).

"No instrument, vessel, or weapon that is trying to squeeze me into another image or form that I wasn't destined to become will make any progress or be effective. Every slanderous, babbling, or accusing word that tries to come on the scene by unlawful entry will depart condemned by its own actions. This is a portion of the inheritance to every bond-servant, laborer, worshipper whose conduct and character stays true before the Lord," (Isa. 54:17, Apostle Hughes paraphrase).

## Chapter Five Reflections

How does this parable speak and/or apply to me?

_____

_____

_____

_____

_____

_____

_____

_____

_____

_____

Action Steps:

What actions should I take today, this week, this month to apply these principles?

_____

_____

_____

_____

_____

_____

_____

_____

_____

_____

_____

_____

_____

_____

_____

_____

Date/Time that these actions were completed?

_____
_____
_____
_____
_____
_____
_____
_____

Closure:

Thoughts, feelings and emotions from these completed actions?

_____
_____
_____
_____
_____
_____
_____
_____
_____
_____
_____
_____
_____
_____
_____
_____
_____

# Chapter Six

# The Net

THIS PARABLE HAS some things worthy of noting as we look at it through Kingdom eyes: *Again, the kingdom of heaven is like unto a net, that was cast into the sea, and gathered of every kind: Which, when it was full, they drew to shore, and sat down, and gathered the good into vessels, but cast the bad away. So shall it be at the end of the world: the angels shall come forth, and sever the wicked from among the just, and shall cast them into the furnace of fire: there shall be wailing and gnashing of teeth,"* (Matt. 13:47-50).

Jesus illustrates the Kingdom as a net which was cast into the sea. Prophetically, the sea can represent humanity. The word "net" translates as a large fishing net or dragnet. Our net should be reaching out to "every kind" (verse 47) every nation, every tribe, every tongue. A true Kingdom mindset is concerned about reaching the world, not just a race, our race, our peoples or even our own gender. It doesn't care about adding to a denomination; it cares about adding to God's family. The word "kind" is the Greek word *"genos"* (pronounced *gheno-os*), which describes nations, offspring, races, and families. Remember: It is not God's will that any (nation, offspring, race or family) perish.

*"The Lord is not slack concerning his promise, as some men count slackness; but is longsuffering to us-ward, not willing that any should perish, but that all should come to repentance,"* (2 Pet. 3:9).

The call has come forth from Jesus Himself that we become *fishers of men. "And he saith unto them, follow me, and I will make you fishers of men,"* (Matt. 4:19).

One of the church's downfalls is that it has become very selective in its fishing, just like men in the natural. If you talk to most *natural* fishermen, they only like to fish for one, maybe two, different types of fish (example: bass, crappie, catfish, striper, etc.). God wants all fish (humanity) reached by His people.

This parable refers to the net becoming full, then division and separation following. I believe there is a dual application here in this parable, and I will explain in more detail as we go further in this chapter. Notice that the good (verse 48) remains; it is the bad that is removed. Good is a reference to something that is excellent because of its nature and characteristics, useful and well-adapted to its specific end. The more of *Gods' good* that grows and expands in us, the less room there will be for the *bad*; that is removed and is cast away.

All too often, in reading a parable like this, we begin to define the story through our denominational upbringing, our own doctrinal beliefs or even what we learned in Sunday School. However, if our understanding is limited, then so will the revelation be also. Do we dare to venture outside the box of our own understanding? Do we dare look at the scriptures with an open mind?

For example...Most read this parable considering its subject matter as simply two types of people, the *good* and the *bad* (verse 48). Have you ever considered that it can be a story about two things happening in the life of one individual? Let me explain: The word "angels" in verse 49 is the Greek word "*aggelos*" (pronounced *ang-el-os)*, which is not ONLY a reference to a heavenly angelic being; it also describes any messenger or envoy (representative, ambassador) sent from and speaking for God. God has many present-day *angels* (men and women of God, five-fold ministry gifts, revealing his truths, plans, and purposes to His people. (See Eph. 4:11-13).

In this parable, the angel's (messenger's) assignment is to "...sever the wicked from among the just" (verse 49). The word "sever" is the Greek word "*aphorize*" (pronounced *af-or-id-zo*), which means "to separate, to divide, and to mark off from others by boundaries." God still has some angels (messengers) today just as He did in Elijah's day who haven't bowed their knees to political church correctness, those who are not afraid to reveal what the Spirit is saying *present-day* to the church, who are seasoned enough to share what the body NEEDS to hear, not just what they WANT to hear.

There are still those who aren't concerned with popular opinion; those more concerned about obeying God than pleasing men.

*"Then Peter and the [other] apostles answered and said, we ought to obey God rather than men,"* (Acts 5:29).

*"Lord, they have killed thy prophets, and digged down thine alters; and I am left alone, and they seek my life. But what saith the answer of God unto him? I have reserved to myself seven thousand men, who have not bowed the knee to [the image of] Baal,"* (Rom. 11:3-4).

What are these angels (messengers) using to sever the good from the bad within us individually and corporately? First and foremost, these messengers must be true students of HIS WORD, not students of the doctrines or traditions of men. We as messengers can't "rightly divide" what we don't understand.

*"Study to shew thyself approved unto God, a workman that needeth not to be ashamed, rightly dividing the word of truth,"* (2 Tim. 2:15).

The word "study" describes someone who is laborious, one who exerts great diligence in their endeavor. The sign of a true student is the ability to rightly divide truth. "Rightly divide" is the Greek word *"orthotomeo"* (pronounced *or-thot-om-eh-o*), which reveals "someone who cuts straight, proceeds on straight paths, holds a straight course, and teaches truth directly and correctly." I have seen many minister's over the last few years leave their love of God's Word and study to present messages that are shallow, non-challenging with no conviction (sad, but true). They have become professional "ear ticklers" because it draws the crowds and keep the money coming in.

*"For the time will come when they will not endure sound doctrine; but after their own lusts shall they heap to themselves teachers, having itching ears,"* (2 Tim. 4:3).

*"For the time will come when men will not tolerate sound doctrine, but with itching ears they will gather around themselves teachers who suit their own desires,"* (2 Tim. 4:3, Berean Study Bible).

*"The time is coming when people won't listen to good teaching. Instead, they will look for teachers who will please them by telling them only what they are itching to hear,"* (2 Tim. 4:3, Contemporary English Version).

His true messengers (angels) are using the two-edged scalpel of God's Word: *"For the word of God [is] quick, and powerful, and sharper than any two-edged sword, piercing even to the dividing asunder of soul and spirit, and of the joints and marrow, and [is] a discerner of the thoughts and intents of the heart,"* (Heb. 4:12).

*"Think not that I am come to send peace on earth: I came not to send peace, but a sword. For I am come to set a man at variance with his father, and the daughter against her mother, and the daughter in law against her mother in law. And a man's foes [shall be] they of his own household,"* (Matt. 10:34-36).

I believe His angels are preaching present-day truth, bringing division, creating a chasm, a separation between HIS WORD and religious rhetoric. These truths are separating the chaff from the wheat.

*"Whose fan [is] in his hand, and he will thoroughly purge his floor, and gather his wheat into the garner; but he will burn up the chaff with unquenchable fire,"* (Matt. 3:12).

They are separating the works of the flesh . . . *"Now the works of the flesh are manifest, which are these; Adultery, fornication, uncleanness, lasciviousness, Idolatry, witchcraft, hatred, variance, emulations, wrath, strife, seditions, heresies, envyings, murders, drunkenness, revellings, and such like: of the which I tell you before, as I have also told you in time past, that they which do such things shall not inherit the kingdom of God,"* (Gal. 5:19-21). . . by living in and operating in the fruit of the Spirit.

*"But the fruit of the Spirit is love, joy, peace, longsuffering, gentleness, goodness, faith, meekness, temperance: against such there is no law. And they that are Christ's have crucified the flesh with the affections and lusts. If we live in the Spirit, let us also walk in the Spirit. Let us not be desirous of vain glory, provoking one another, envying one another,"* (Gal. 5:22-26).

The wheat is being separated from the tares (refer to chapter one). All of these examples of flesh listed above are things that can be at work in of each of us right now. It is the sword (God's WORD) that will bring proper division in our house (temple, tabernacle).

Look again at Matthew 10:36, *"And a man's foes [shall be] they of his own household."*

I want you to pay close attention to the words "own household" in verse 36. Yes, I realize the reference here includes a "family within a household" divided over things being revealed; however, it goes even deeper. The word "own" is the Greek word "autos" (pronounced *ow-tos*); the word "household" is the Greek word "*oikiakos*" (pronounced *oy-kee-ak-os*)

Together, they describe an individual, male or female, living in an edifice, a dwelling place, a tabernacle, the house of God. It is also a reference to the human body (Thayer's #3624). Let us bring this closer to home (not a play on words), it speaks of the sword removing anything *within us* that has the potential to bring about corruption (Matt.13:48).

I believe also that the application is here to remove generational things passed down through family (father, mother, etc.).

In closing this chapter, let's look again at the last two verses in this parable. Matthew 13:49-50. Verse 49 reveals God's messengers severing the "wicked" from the "just." *Wicked* is the Greek word *"poneros" (pronounced pon-ay-ros)*, which portrays something diseased, blind, in bad condition or of a bad nature. These heaven-sent messengers are shearing off (severing with the sword of the Spirit) anything and everything that can affect God's vessels from becoming and producing all that He has ordained for them. Remember God's armor in Ephesians 6.

*"...and the sword of the Spirit, which is the word of God:"* (Eph.6:17).

Another thought to ponder is the definition of this word "wicked." These words define wicked: annoyances, hardships, things that have brought toils, perils, pain and trouble. In other words, many of the hardships, pain, trouble and difficulty that we face could be headed off or removed by removing or uprooting the seed that causes them. God's word is dealing with our *disease,* our spiritual blindness, and He wants us to use His sword to cut away every internal thing that impacts our external walk. Notice also in verse 49 that the *wicked* are among the just.

The Greek word for "among" is "*mesos*" (pronounced *mes-os*) and speaks of something "in the midst of, in the middle of." These bad things that need removing are in the midst or middle of. It would do us some good to remind ourselves again of the words of the Apostle Paul to the Church in Rome.

*"For I know that in me (that is, in my flesh), dwelleth no good thing: for to will is present with me; but [how] to perform that which is good I find not. 19 For the good that I would I do not: but the evil which I would not, that I do. Now if I do that I would not, it is no more I that do it, but sin dwelleth in me. I find then a law, that, when I would do good, evil is present with me. For I delight in the law of God after the inward man: But I see another law in my members, warring against the law of my mind, and bringing me into captivity to the law of sin which is in my members. O wretched man that I am! who shall deliver me from the body of this death? I thank God through Jesus Christ our Lord. So then with my mind I myself serve the law of God; but with the flesh the law of sin,"* (Rom. 7:18-25).

Thank God for the transparent preacher willing to reveal his own internal struggles between "good and bad," but then also revealing the key to victory. In the very next chapter Paul reveals the answer to overcoming this "war within our members" (See Rom. 8). The Spirit within each of us wants to remove the *wicked* within that can affect the *just* within.

The word "just" can be translated as "righteous; that which keeps the commands of God; those whose feelings, actions, and thinking are wholly conformed to the will of God." Every sheep needs a shepherd, every son needs a father, every congregation needs an angel (messenger) to rightly divide truth, so nothing hinders our destiny, purpose, and calling.

Just a thought for all the eschatology buffs, those with their bags packed, sitting on their *blessed assurance*, doing nothing (well...there are many that fit this description), waiting, waiting, and waiting! If you are one that thinks this parable is only about two groups of people, the "wicked" and the "just," did you notice that the wicked are "severed" (removed) from the "just," not the other way around? JUST A THOUGHT!

God's angels (messengers) are wielding the sword of the Spirit and severing things within us that need to be removed. Even in the final verse of this parable, another interesting thought comes forth for our consideration:

*"And shall cast them into the furnace of fire: there shall be wailing and gnashing of teeth,"* (Matt. 13:50).

God IS NOT into disfigurement; He doesn't want to disfigure you and I. His Word through His angels is simply taking everything that is earthen, fleshly and uncommitted, into the fire of His presence for purification.

*"For our God [is] a consuming fire,'* (Heb. 12:29).

*"That the trial of your faith, being much more precious that of gold that perisheth, though it be tried with fired, might be found unto praise and honour and glory at the appearing of Jesus Christ,"* (1 Pet. 1:7).

*"Behold, I have refined thee, but not with silver; I have chosen thee in the furnace of affliction,"* (Isa. 48:10).

The word "furnace" is referring to something used for "burning earthenware." You and I are referred to in scripture as "earthen vessels."

*"But we have this treasure in earthen vessels, that the excellency of the power may be of God, and not of us,"* (2 Cor. 4:7).

The words "wailing" and "gnashing" describe an individual mourning over things that are dying or that have died. You know that OLD HABITS DIE HARD; we like our flesh and it appetites. We know they have to go; they have to be dealt with. It is literally time, as the old Pentecostal preachers would say to "LET GO AND LET GOD."

## Chapter Six Reflections

How does this parable speak and/or apply to me?

_____

_____

_____

_____

_____

_____

_____

_____

_____

_____

_____

_____

Action Steps:

What actions should I take today, this week, this month to apply these principles?

_____

_____

_____

_____

_____

_____

_____

_____

_____

_____

_____

_____

_____

Date/Time that these actions were completed?

_____

_____

_____

_____

_____

_____

_____

Closure:

Thoughts, feeling and emotions from these completed actions?

_____

_____

_____

_____

_____

_____

_____

_____

_____

_____

_____

_____

_____

_____

_____

_____

_____

# CHAPTER SEVEN

# THE HOUSEHOLDER

THIS NEXT PARABLE, which describes the kingdom of heaven is the householder. *"Jesus saith unto them, Have ye understood all these thing? They say unto him, Yea, Lord. Then said he unto them, Therefore every scribe [which is] instructed unto the kingdom of heaven is like unto a man [that is] an householder, which bringeth forth out of his treasure [thing] new and old. And it came to pass [that] when Jesus had finished these parables, he departed thence,"* (Matt. 13:51-53).

Jesus begins this kingdom parable with a question: "Have you *understood* all these things?" In the Greek language, He is asking His disciples if they had "joined their mind to" (Greek *"suniemi"*, pronounced *soon-ee-ay-mee*), had they truly perceived, the parables/principles He had expounded upon. He didn't ask them if they *heard,* He asked them if they *understood,* they are not the same. There is a big difference! There are several references in the New Testament that state "they understood *not"* the things Jesus was speaking.

Examples:

*"But they understood not that saying, and were afraid to ask him,"* (Mark 9:32).

*"And they understood not the saying which he spake unto them,"* (Luke 2:50).

*"But they understood not this saying, and it was hid from them, that they perceived it not: and they feared to ask him of that saying,"* (Luke 9:45).

*"And they understood none of these things: and this saying was hid from them, neither knew they the things which were spoken,"* (Luke 18:34).

*"They understood not that he spake to them of the Father,"* (John 8:27).

This kingdom parable is a prophetic illustration instructing men/women to write, declare and decree the principles of the kingdom. The Greek word for "scribe" is *"grammateus"* (pronounced *gram-mat-yooce*), which describes a clerk, a recorder and an interpreter of the Mosaic Law and sacred writings.

It also refers to a religious teacher. You can't pen what you haven't heard, seen or done. God is raising up and releasing men and women who have been through the school of the Holy Ghost, those hidden on the back side of nowhere, those who choose to preach present-day truth (what the Spirit has revealed to them in their wilderness times and is being declared NOW, TODAY), regardless of religious opinion. They aren't concerned with being popular or even accepted by today's religious, man-centered, watered-down gospel, seeker-friendly churches. And by the way, many of these types of people that I have met aren't seeking HIM, and they sure aren't FRIENDLY...Selah.

There is a line of an old secular (I know this will upset some, too) song that describes their mindset: "Don't rock the boat, baby, don't tip the boat over."

Those who have received, learned and/or are learning these kingdom principles have been "instructed," the Greek word *"matheteuo"* (pronounced *math-ayt-yoo-o*), to reveal these truths. The word describes a person who follows the precepts and instructions learned, thus making disciples increase in their knowledge to a greater and fuller understanding of these truths. This parable identifies the revealer of information as the "householder," the Greek word *"oikodespotes"* (pronounced *oy-kod-es-pot-ace*), which denotes a "master of the house, a husband, the head of the house of God."

This is a reference to the man/woman of God who is responsible for feeding, instructing, exhorting and admonishing the body of Christ. There ae kingdom truths being revealed today by those "householders' that is changing the church from a lethargic, complacent and impotent house into the powerful instrument through which God's kingdom can be seen. Neighborhoods, cities, regions, states, nations and governments are being and will be affected.

Jesus uses the word "treasure" to describe what the householder is bringing forth today. Treasure if the Greek word *"thesauros"* (pronounced *thay-sow-ros*), which portrays a place in which good and precious things are collected or laid up. It also refers to a storehouse. In Matthew 13:52, Jesus uses the phrase "...out of *his* treasure..." referring to whom? The householders! It can't be *your treasure* unless *you* found it. You can't "find" treasure you aren't "searching" for. It is our responsibility as "householders" to search for these good and precious things that God wants revealed to the world. I am reminded of the scripture that says:

*"Blessed [are] they which do hunger and thirst after righteousness: for they shall be filled,"* (Matt. 5:6)

These treasures are revealing both new and old. "New" is the Greek word *"kainos"* (pronounced *kahee-nos*), which translates as "fresh, unworn, uncommon and unheard of things." The word "old" simply describes a "renewal of the former things." God's householders are bringing forth fresh manna, things that are uncommon (unheard of to the traditional religious mindset), treasure that is alive and relevant to today's issues. These householders also understand that they must continually remind God's people of the former things they may have let slip in their Christian walk (prayer, forgiveness, giving, fasting, etc.). Here are some promises concerning "old and new" things:

*"Behold, the former things are come to pass, and new things do I declare: before they spring forth I tell you of them,"* (Isa. 42:9)

*"Remember the former things of old: for I [am] God, and [there is] none else; [I am] God, and [there is] none like me, Declaring the end from the beginning, and from ancient times [the things] that are not [yet] done, saying, My counsel shall stand, and I will do all my pleasure,"* (Isa. 46:9-10).

*"I have declared the former things from the beginning; and they went forth out of my mouth, and I shewed them; I did [them] suddenly, and they came to pass,"* (Isa. 48:3).

The former and the new are both important; one simply gives way or precedes the other. The prophet Haggai stated that the "glory of the latter house shall be greater than of the former."

*"The glory of this latter house shall be greater than of the former, saith the LORD of hosts: and in this place will I give peace, saith the LORD of hosts,"* (Hag.2:9).

They are both needed; one is just released in a greater measure. Ecclesiastes didn't say the beginning wasn't important, just that the end was better:

*"Better [is] the end of a thing than the beginning thereof..."* (Eccl. 7:8).

Attention all householders, great and small, red, yellow, black, and white, male and female, young and old: There is treasure yet to be found, thus yet to be revealed. Get back into the Word of God, renew the joy of your salvation. There are people whose destinies depend upon the treasure that you will find and reveal. Ask Holy Spirit to reveal every religious hindrance, every old mindset that would keep the veil from being removed. No longer can we afford to look (see) through a glass darkly.

*"For now we see through a glass, darkly; but then face to face: now I know part; but then shall I know even as also I am known,"* (1 Cor. 13:12).

I believe present-day revelation is being revealed at a rate paralleling modern technology, if not even quicker.

Who has an ear to hear?

*"He that hath an ear, let him hear what the Spirit saith unto the churches,"* (Rev. 2:7b).

Who has a single eye to see?

*"The light of the body is the eye: if therefore thine eye be single, they whole body shall be full of light,"* (Matt. 6:22).

*"The eye is the lamp of the body. If your vision is clear, your whole body will be full of light,"* (Matt. 6:22, BSB).

Our earth (vessel) has groaned and quaked, desiring the manifestation of the true sons of God. This has produced a tsunami of spiritual revelation moving in the direction to cover the earth (us) with God's glory. It's moving your direction: Are you ready?

## Chapter Seven Reflections

How does this parable speak and/or apply to me?

_____

_____

_____

_____

_____

_____

_____

_____

_____

_____

_____

_____

Actions Steps:

What actions should I take today, this week, this month to apply these
principles?

_____

_____

_____

_____

_____

_____

_____

_____

_____

_____

_____

_____

Date/Time these actions were completed?

_____

_____

_____

_____

_____

_____

_____

_____

Closure:

Thoughts, feelings and emotions from these completed actions?

_____

_____

_____

_____

_____

_____

_____

_____

_____

_____

_____

_____

_____

_____

_____

_____

_____

_____

# CHAPTER EIGHT

# THE KING'S SERVANTS

THIS KINGDOM PARABLE is *one of the most important* ever ministered by the Lord. This kingdom principle can never be OVEREMPHASIZED. It is the principle that, if lived by, will manifest a long, productive, and fruitful life. In a nutshell, the parable/principle deals with the concept of FORGIVENESS. Jesus begins to explain this parable in Matthew 18:23-35 in response to a question presented by Peter two verses earlier. Note Peter's question in Matthew 18:21-22:

*"Then came Peter to him, and said, Lord, how oft shall my brother sin against me, and I forgive him? Till seven times: Jesus saith unto him, I say not unto thee, until seven times: but, until seventy times seve."*

Peter's question actually was preceded by Jesus' instruction in Matthew 18:15-20 where He established the procedure of dealing with a brother who "trespasses against us."

*"Moreover if they brother shall trespass against thee, go and tell him his fault between thee and him alone: if he shall hear thee, thou hast gained thy brother. But if he will not hear [thee, then] take with thee one or two more, that in the mouth of two or three witnesses every word may be established. And if he shall neglect to hear them, tell [it] unto the church: but if he neglect to hear the church, let him be unto thee as an heathen man and a publican. Verily I say unto you, whatsoever ye shall bind on earth shall be bound in heaven: and whatsoever ye shall loose on earth shall be loosed in heaven. Again I say unto you, that if two of you shall agree on earth as touching any thing that they shall ask, it shall be done for them of my Father which is in heaven. For where two or three are gather together in my name, there am I in the midst of them,"* (Matt. 18:15-20).

In these six verses, He breaks down the progression of biblically and correctly dealing with a brother that has "ought against thee." I can just see Apostle Peter as he intently listens as Jesus expounds this kingdom principle of forgiveness. Any student of God's Word knows Peters' reputation with "open mouth, insert foot and chew" (Boy, can I relate to him!) His question presented to Jesus in verses 21-22 had nothing to do with some formula of "celestial arithmetic." I believe that Peter's question to Jesus was revealing his heart condition, his point of no return, the limit he was willing to forgive a brother, and possibly hoping he would impress the Master with the "seven times."

True forgiveness has everything to do with our CONDUCT and ATTITUDE in the process. I believe Peter had calculated already in his mind his level of forgiveness, the most he could allow himself to forgive, as stated about, his point of no return. Jesus' response was not because he had a bigger calculator (verse 22). He was revealing that His "ways and thoughts are higher than ours."

*"For my thoughts [are] not your thoughts, neither [are] your ways my ways, saith the LORD. For [as] the heavens are higher than the earth, so are my ways higher than your ways, and my thoughts than your thoughts,"* (Isa. 55:8-9).

However, for all of you analytical junkies (LOL), let me break it down for you:

Peter said, "… seven times."

Jesus said "… seventy times seven."

70 X 7 = 490. One of the four gospels references forgiving daily. There are 24 hours in every day. The average person sleeps about 8 hours each day, leaving 16 hours to forgive someone (even if it's the same person) 490 times. Let me break it down even further: That is forgiveness being activated and/or released every 90 seconds. The number nine (9) in the Bible represents "finality and also birth." True forgiveness can bring closure to things that need closed and birth something new and fresh. The bottom line is this: It's not a formula.

IT IS A WAY OF LIFE; FORGIVENESS IS A PRINCIPLE OF LIFE. Some of the definitions for the word *forgive* are to "dismiss; release; no longer discuss; send away from; release from bondage so that one if free/restored; to completely cancel the debt.

*True forgiveness happens when we forget and hold NO GRUDGES.*

The Lord showed me this principle on one occasion as I was looking at my personal credit report. I had found a discrepancy on my report that showed a *bad debt* had been *written off*, and yet still remained on my report. Even though it had been "written off," seemingly "forgiven," it still was a derogatory remark against my credit score, thus affecting my ability to purchase. (Are you seeing the prophetic implications?) I researched the discrepancy, found it to be inaccurate and disputed the matter with the credit reporting agency. Thirty days later, I received an updated copy of the report. This time, the bad debt that had been "written off" had also been "REMOVED." My credit score increased; thus, my ability to purchase at the best rates was available again. (Are you getting the picture?) SELAH.

he kind of forgiveness that Jesus is referring to in this parable is a "forgive and forget" forgiveness; it is a "written off and removed" forgiveness. The word "forgive" actually means to "FORTH-GIVE" to dismiss absolutely from thought. When we "forth-give" someone, we are releasing them from the weight of a matter, not just the words, but ACTIONS, ultimately removing it from our thoughts as though it never happened. That is God's way of doing things.

The people of God's kingdom MUST UNDERSTAND and OPERATE in this type of forgiveness. However, this level of forgiveness can only be accomplished in HIS strength and through HIS nature. When we ignore this principle, knowingly or unknowingly, we put ourselves and the debtor in bondage. All too often in ministering to people with unforgiveness, they want to just *deal with the symptoms*. Yet God's desire is to get to the ROOT (the internals, the things not easily seen) of the problem. Things cut off at the surface grow back (and seemingly at an alarming rate); things uprooted are removed permanently, unless replanted.

Now, let's break down the parable that Jesus taught in Matthew 18:23-35:

*"Therefore is the kingdom of heaven likened unto a certain king, which would take account of his servants. And when he had begun to reckon, one was brought unto him, which owed him ten thousand talents. But forasmuch as he had not to pay, his lord commanded him to be sold, and his wife, and children, and all that he had, and payment to be made. The servant therefore fell down, and worshipped him, saying, Lord, have patience with me, and I will pay thee all. Then the lord of that servant was moved with compassion, and loosed him, and forgave him the debt. But the same servant went out, and found one of his fellowservants, which owed him an hundred pence: and he laid hands on him, and took [him] by the throat, saying, Pay me that thou owest. And his fellowservant fell down at his feet, and besought him, saying, Have patience with me, and I will pay thee all. And he would not: but went and cast him into prison, till he should pay the debt. So when his fellowservants saw what was done, they were very sorry, and came and told unto their lord all that was done. Then his lord after that he had called him, said unto him, O thou wicked servant, I forgave thee all that debt, because thou desiredst me: Shouldest not thou also have had compassion on thy fellowservant, even as I had pity of thee? And his lord was wroth, and delivered him to the tormentors, till he should pay all that was due unto him. So likewise shall my heavenly Father do also unto you, if ye from your hearts forgive not every one his brother their trespasses."*

It begins with the king realizing that one of his servants owed him ten thousand talents. From my calculations, along with what I have heard others say over the years, this equates to approximately twenty million ($20,000,000.00) dollars. I trust that you see the prophetic implication of this amount is insurmountable, it's a no way-out number; it was a figure in the natural that was so far out of reach and without hope of repayment. It was very common in ancient times that the debtor would be sold into slavery for the debt owed; and if the debt was extremely large, often the wife and children would be sold also.

In verse 26, the servant asks the king to be patient (long suffering); this describes one of the attributes of Father God.

*"The LORD [is] longsuffering, and of great mercy, forgiving iniquity and transgression,"* (Numb. 14:18a).

*"But thou, O Lord, [art] a God full on compassion, and gracious, longsuffering, and plenteous in mercy and truth,"* (Ps. 86:15).

*"But the fruit of the Spirit is love, joy, peace, longsuffering, gentleness, faith,"* (Gal. 5:22).

In verse 27 of the parable, it states that the lord was "moved with compassion" towards his servant. It literally means that he was moved from the bowels (Greek word *"splagchnizomai"* pronounced *splangkh-nid-zom-ahee*). In those days, the bowels were thought of to be the seat of love, pity and tender affections. Something else to consider is that one of the other Greek words or compassion is where we get out English word "spleen" from. The spleen filters the blood and removes abnormal cells (unforgiveness could be called an abnormal cell). It also makes disease fighting components of the immune system, including antibodies.

Giving and receiving forgiveness is essential for your health and the health of others. When the lord was moved with compassion, he was moved *internally*, which manifested *externally*. What a level of forgiveness released, an insurmountable sum of debt forgiven! Look at the NATURE OF THE KING.

In verse 28, the forgiven servant leaves the presence of the forgiving king and runs into one of his fellow servants, the Greek word for servants is *"sundoulos"* (pronounced *soon-doo-los*), which describes one who serves the same master with another. You would almost automatically think that one who has been forgiven MUCH would quickly be willing to forgive LITTLE. NOT SO! His fellow servant owed him about twenty dollars ($20.00). The Bible says in verse 28 that he (his fellow servant) "took him by the throat" literally began to wring his neck over a twenty dollar ($20.00) debt. For those analytical folks, twenty dollars ($20) is .001% (which is 1/1000$^{th}$ of 1%) of twenty million dollars ($20,000,000.00).

The servant asked his fellow servant who had been extended mercy and received incredible forgiveness from the king to extend the same, and it was refused. He cast his associate into prison over twenty dollars. The MUCH forgiven servant was referred to in the parable as a "wicked servant." The word "wicked" is the Greek word *"poneros"* (pronounced *pon-ay-os*), which describes someone whose *nature is bad.* The king had released this servant of that tremendous, unpayable debt just because he had asked. However, his nature would not allow him to release the same forgiveness.

In verse 34, the king turns the "wicked servant" over to the tormentors. WHY? He didn't pass the test. One of the derivative words for "tormentors" is the Greek word "*basanizo*" (pronounced *bas-an-id-zo*), describing a stone (by the way, the Bible refers to us as "lively stones") which is rubbed against gold or silver to test the purity. Be careful of your response when someone "rubs you the wrong way." Their action doesn't require a negative reaction from you. What color do you manifest when provoked, when evil is spoken of you, when talked about, etc.? Verse 35 sums up this parable/principle by stating that forgiveness must be from the heart, the internal/unseen realm. This is not a *lip-service* forgiveness; it is from the place that is considered the seat of all spiritual and physical life. Kingdom forgiveness is demonstrated by *removing* the unforgiveness from the internals, the heart, the thoughts, the mouth and eventually *seen* externally by our actions.

One thought in closing: The "wicked servant" was turned over to the tormentors over twenty dollars ($20), NOT twenty millions dollars ($20,000,000.00). Many are in spiritual chains and prison today, not because of the big things, but over the twenty dollar decisions. Selah (Think on this)!

On a Personal Note: Forgiveness released...Warts Gone

In my early pre-teen years, one day I overheard my grandmother speaking ill of my father to my mother. Out of my adolescent ignorance, I stood before my grandmother and told her that I hated her and never wanted to see her again, and then left the room hastily.

Several years later, I was married, had my own family, graduated Bible school and was traveling the nation, ministering the good news of the gospel. Warts began to appear on both my hands, and over a few months there were more than a dozen. I started confessing all the healing scriptures that I knew and had been taught, to no avail. I was embarrassed by them, and at times, in much pain.

There I was, God's man of faith and power, traveling the country and preaching the gospel. People were being saved, healed and delivered, and I couldn't conquer these warts. So, I went to "plan B" (you know what I mean, when things don't seem to be working and we try our own thing) and purchased *Compound W*, literally bottles of it, still to no avail! I cursed them, I bound them, I loosed them, I tried to cut them off (dumb idea), and nothing worked. Finally, I had a revelation that, if nothing was working, maybe I should ask God as to why.

In prayer, the answer came quickly. All of a sudden I saw myself in my grandmother's room years earlier, watching the situation unfold again, and I heard my voice saying, "I hate you, and I never want to see you again." The Lord spoke to me and stated that my "unforgiveness" had opened the door to these warts that were plaguing me. I immediately asked His forgiveness, contacted my grandmother, and shared the story with her. I asked her forgiveness, and within thirty days, every wart had disappeared, without even a scar. As my late father, Dr. Don Hughes Sr. use to say, "The Word works when you work the Word."

Whatever it was, whoever it was…It isn't worth it!

Forgive them, release it and watch God begin to work in and through your life.  Remember; it is the goodness of God that leads men to repentance. You be CHRIST-like and watch the brass heavens open up, and the blessings of the Lord once again begin to flow to and through you

*"Our despisest thou the riches of his goodness and forbearance and longsuffering; not knowing that the goodness of God leadeth thee to repentance?"* (Rom. 2:4).

The opposite of "goodness" are words like "harsh, hard, sharp and bitter." People that manifest God's goodness are those who are virtuous, kind, gracious and benevolent. The word "goodness" actually is the Greek word *"christos"* which is a derivative of the word CHRIST. Our Christ-likeness will lead others to real repentance. When we think like Christ, we will act like Christ.

Here is the acid-test to your testimony. You're words and actions are producing what? Have you ever heard this statement in response to your words or actions? "If that is what being a Christian is all about, if that what they are teaching at your church…no thank you?" Selah!

### Chapter Eight Reflections

How does this parable speak and/or apply to me?

_____

_____

_____

_____

_____

_____

_____

_____

_____

_____

_____

_____

_____

Action Steps:

What actions should I take today, this week, this month to apply these principles?

_____

_____

_____

_____

_____

_____

_____

_____

_____

_____

_____

_____

Date/Time that these actions were completed?

_____

_____

_____

_____

_____

_____

_____

Closure:

Thoughts, feelings and emotions from these completed actions?

_____

_____

_____

_____

_____

_____

_____

_____

_____

_____

_____

_____

# CHAPTER NINE

# THE MARRIAGE FEAST

THIS KINGDOM PARABLE has great prophetic significance. It begins in Matthew 22 and is expounded upon for fourteen verses: *"And Jesus answered and spake unto them again by parables, and said, the kingdom of heaven is like unto a certain king, which made a marriage for his son, and sent forth his servants to call them that were bidden to the wedding: and they would not come. Again, he sent forth other servants, saying Tell them which are bidden, Behold, I have prepared my dinner: my oxen and [my] fatlings [are] killed, and all things [are] ready: come unto the marriage. But they made light of [it], and went their ways, one to his farm, another to his merchandise: And the remnant took his servants, and entreated [them] spitefully, and slew them]. But when the king heard [thereof], he was wroth: and he sent forth armies, and destroyed those murderers, and burned up their city. Then saith he to his servants, the wedding is ready, but they which were bidden were not worthy. Go ye therefore into the highways, and as many as ye shall find, bid to the marriage. So those servants went out into the highways, and gathered together all as many as they found, both bad and good: and the wedding was furnished with guests. And when the king came in to see the guests, he saw there a man which had not on a wedding garment: And he saith unto him, Friend, how comest thou hither not having a wedding garment? And he was speechless. Then said the king to the servants, Bind him hand and foot and take him away, and cast [him] into outer darkness; there shall be weeping and gnashing of teeth. For many are called, but few [are] chosen,"* (Matt. 22:1-14).

This "certain" king prepares a wedding banquet, literally, a wedding feast on behalf of his son. Just imagine: The room was prepared with the finest linens, 100% Egyptian cotton. Each setting was the finest china available, and the eating utensils were 24K gold, placed precisely beside one another. The crystal glasses sparkled under the lights and the napkins were creased and folded to perfection. The chef had been preparing his delicacies for hours from scratch, using only the best ingredients, vegetables, meat, fish and poultry that were available. Everything was in place for the greatest meal yet to be consumed; however, something essential was missing: PEOPLE! Let's dissect this kingdom story as Jesus delivers this parable.

In this parable, the king sends forth his "servants" to invite the guests to the celebration. The Greek word for "servant" is *"doulos"* (pronounced *doo-los*), which describes one who gives himself up to another's will, those who service is used by Christ in extending and advancing His cause. These represent those men and women who have answered the call, given their lives and will to do Christ's bidding. I believe, prophetically, they represent the ministry gifts mentioned in Ephesians.

*"And he gave some, apostles; and some, pastors and teachers; 12 For the perfecting of the saints, for the work of the ministry, for the edifying of the body of Christ: 13 Till we all come in the unity of faith, and of the knowledge of the Son of God, unto a perfect man, unto the measure of the stature of the fullness of Christ,"* (Eph.4:11-13).

The responsibility of God's servants is to announce the celebration, to *bid* those to come who have been invited. Who does that include? The word "bidden" is the Greek word *"kaleo"* (pronounced *kal-eh-o*), which refers to those who have been "given the name of, given a name to; those who call upon His name, or those who bear a name or title." As God's servants, His gifts to men, we have been sent forth to bid all those to come to this celebration of covenant, food and fellowship. The guest list is all those who have received the Name, called upon or bear His name.

The first invitation by the king's servants made no impact upon the invited guests. Notice closely in verse 3 that it states "they would not come." There is a major difference between the phrases *would not* and *could not*. The king sends out his servants a second time with specific instructions to tell those bidden that "I have *prepared* my dinner." The word *prepared* is the Greek word *"hetoimazo"* (pronounced *het-oy-mad-zo*). This word defines as "made ready; made the necessary preparations." This word is drawn from an Asian custom of sending persons on before a king's journeying to level the roads, remove obstacles and make them passable. It also refers to preparing the minds of men to give the Messiah a fit reception and to secure His blessings. The call has gone forth for God's gifts (His servants) to prepare the road for life's journey, to prepare the bidden guests for a reception in honor of our Messiah.

The King James Bible refers to the meal as *dinner*, however, this is misleading with our cultures understanding of the word *dinner*. The word *dinner* is the Greek word *"ariston"* (pronounced *ar-is-ton*), describing the first food taken in the morning before work; literally, breakfast. It was the breakfast *of* and *for* champions. Those who partake become champions. Those who don't...WELL!

The people's response to the invitation the second time was much like the first; they made light of it. Simply stated, they disregarded, neglected and could care less. Why? Verse 5 says they "went their ways" continuing to do their *own thing*. Have we become so complacent with the things of God that we have forgotten scriptures like these?

*"There is a way that seemeth right unto a man, but the end thereof [are] the ways of death,"* (Prov.16:25).

*"For my thoughts [are] not your thoughts, neither [are] your ways my ways, saith the LORD. For [as] the heavens are higher than the earth, so are my ways higher than your ways, and my thoughts than your thoughts,"* (Isa. 55:8-9).

Don't forget the kingdom principle: *"But seek ye first the kingdom of God, and his righteousness; and all these things shall be added unto you,"* (Matt. 6:33).

"First and foremost, in order of importance, be a true worshipper in God's kingdom, the place Messiah reigns, pursue integrity, virtue and purity of life, and then all will be gathered to and accompany you because of your active position of worship," (Apostle Hughes paraphrase).

The Bible says they went their way, one to his farm, another to his merchandise (verse 5). The word "farm" is the Greek word *"agros"* (pronounced *ag-ros*), which is defined as a field, a piece of ground or ones' own country. The word "merchandise" is the Greek word "*emporos*" (pronounced *em-por-os*), which describes a merchant, a trade; however, the most revealing is *a journey that departs from life.*

These people were invited to a great celebration, a covenant celebration involving the king's son, but treated the invitation with disdain, neglect, literally a "not interested, don't bother me" attitude. They were more concerned about their "own field" (flesh) and had become so accustomed to doing their own thing that they now were off course, away from the life that was most important. The remnant (verse 6) took the servants and "entreated them spitefully." The word "remnant" signifies those in lack, destitute and in want. You would have thought that those in lack, destitute and in want would have "gladly received" the word (invitation); yet, the parable states that the remnant "…entreated them spitefully and slew them." The Greek words for "entreated them spitefully" and "slew" reveal some who "injures another by speaking evil of them because of their own pride and haughtiness," someone who "kills in any way, who separates one from another, where the union and fellowship is destroyed." It also refers to those who bring separation to that which has been SET IN ORDER, ORDAINED, APPOINTED, AND ASSIGNED. Set in order and ordained by whom? GOD!

This past generation has shown little reverence for God, let alone His gifts (servants). Rather than looking at their own cause of lack and want, they have spoken evil of those who boldly declare present-day truth. They have brought separation and division among many in God's kingdom. Their own religious pride keeps them from acknowledging that there is more revelation yet to be revealed, more miracles yet to be seen, and more prosperity yet to be released. They still sit empty, dry, and disillusioned in their own little box (mind set, wine skin, or denomination), trying to convince themselves that they have *it all.*

Be very careful in this season about speaking against God's anointed (See 1 Chron. 16:22 and Ps. 105:15). Let me add something right here for clarification, these verses state "my prophet." Today more than ever, especially because of social media, many who have a phone, a living room that has become a pulpit, has become a self-proclaimed prophet, declaring things that

God never said. SELAH! Besides all that falseness and flakiness, be very careful in this season about causing division among the brethren concerning what God IS saying and doing. It could cost you... everything. I pray that a genuine spirit of repentance to be released right now through those who have caused the death and demise of churches, ministers and leadership. May the error of our ways be seen, and let healing and restoration come. REMEMBER: When you mess with the King's messengers (servants), you mess with the King.

The third time the king responds, he sent forth his armies. What were they sent forth to do? To bring an end to division and those who have murdered (with their word and actions) God's gifts (servants). There is a remnant of the soldiers, proven in war, victorious in battle and able to keep rank, those who understand and operate in kingdom authority, a remnant that are about their Father's business, desiring to proclaim and manifest a corporate Christ, NOT those building their own kingdom. They will come with such wisdom, revelation and knowledge. They will come manifesting and demonstrating the kingdom with such an anointing that the religious will be exposed and removed, no longer able to release their man-made doctrines and traditions that have produced a weak, impotent and powerless church. They will come with the fire of God in their mouths, and the revelation of the Christ in their breath will burn all the religious chaff and stubble.

If you don't believe this, you had better re-read Hebrews 1:7, *"And of the angels he saith, who maketh his angels spirits, and his ministers a flame of fire."*

In this parable, the armies burned the city or, literally, the place where the people congregate and dwell. I am not talking about torching literal buildings; I am talking about the revelation that is coming out from God's army that will burn away everything that isn't CHRIST-centered.

Finally, the king sends his servants out, saying, "Forget those who were previously invited; they haven't merited anything and are due NO reward" (literal Greek). Look at the next several verses:

*"Go ye therefore into the highways, and as many as ye shall find, bid to the marriage. So those servants went out into the highways, and gathered together all as many as they found, both bad and good: and the wedding*

*was furnished with guests. And when the king came in to see the guests, he saw there a man which had not on a wedding garment: And he saith unto him, Friend, how camest thou in hither not having a wedding garment? And he was speechless. Then said the king to the servants, Bind him hand and foot, and take him away, and cast [him] into outer darkness; there shall be weeping and gnashing of teeth,"* (Matt. 22:9-13).

The servants are sent into the highways to bring people to the marriage celebration. The word "highways" refers to the roads outside of the city, what we would call country roads. I believe that he was speaking prophetically to go after those who are in the wilderness, those wandering aimlessly, those who have lost their hope of ever reaching their city (destiny) and those the religious have given up on. Some of the greatest apostles, prophets, evangelists, pastors and teachers have yet to enter public ministry. And where many of them are RIGHT NOW would cause religion to never even acknowledge them… BUT GOD!

The servants went after the "good" and "bad." The meal that God is serving today is not reserved for any specific gender, ethnic group, region, denomination or country. It is available to any and all who will come to the table.

Several years ago, I heard of a church in the Bible-belt that had begun to experience a real revival, a genuine move of God. Folks were literally coming into this church from the streets, prostitutes, drug dealer, drug users, the homeless, he young and old, white collar, blue collar, no collar, and the church was exploding, standing room only. They were receiving Christ in record numbers; man were being baptized in the Holy Ghost and then it happened. Some of the money people approached the pastor and stated that they didn't want that type of people in their church; after all, they didn't look like, talk like or smell like them. These so-called Christians told the pastor that these people needed to go or that they (the money people) would leave the church. The pastor escorted them to the front of the church and said they could go and take their money with them. (Oh, I like him) The church continued to grow and expand without financial loss in spite of the money people leaving.

Something happens in this parable in verse 12 that I find quite interesting. In the writing of this manuscript, it took almost two weeks of prayer and meditation concerning the question the kind asked the improperly-clothed man at the wedding before revelation was given to me. In the East, even to this day, is a custom where the wedding host presents each guest with robes of honor. This robe of honor represents reputation, principle, a mark of distinction and most importantly, reverence. I know that there will be those who disagree with me stating that this robe simply represents man's righteousness, which is defined as filthy rags.

*"But we are all an unclean [thing], and all our righteousness [are] filthy rags; and we all do fade as a leaf; and our iniquities, like the wind, have taken us away,"* (Isa. 64:6).

Versus the righteousness of God:

*"For he hath made him [to be] sin for us, who knew no sin; that we might be made the righteousness of God in him,"* (2 Cor. 5:21)

*"And be found in him, not having mine own righteousness, which is of the law, but that which is through the faith of Christ, the righteousness which is of God by faith,"* (Phil. 3:9).

Some will say it represents a man who entered the wedding feast dressed in his own attire and not the garment offered by the host. I can see that in a limited application; however, more is revealed in the light of present-day truth.

The Father is raising up a people in this 3<sup>rd</sup> day (See my book *The 3<sup>rd</sup> Day, The Spirit of Revelation*) that are concerned about manifesting the corporate CHRIST; they are more concerned about being a part of the many membered ekklesia the Body of Christ. They are more concerned about manifesting Christ that is IN them and being released THROUGH them.

*"But put ye on the Lord Jesus Christ, and make not provision for the flesh, to [fulfill] the lusts [thereof],"* (Rom. 13:14).

*"For as many of you as have been baptized into Christ have put on Christ. There is neither Jew nor Greek, there is neither bond nor free, there is neither male nor female; for ye are all one in Christ Jesus,"* (Gal. 3:27-28).

There are a people today who are more committed to displaying the garments of God rather than their Baptist, Methodist, Assembly of God or even Word of Faith (just to name a few) clothing. *Hey, it is about looking like and acting like Him!* I have been preaching forty-three years at the rewriting and revising of this book, and all too often, I can meet a preacher or their peers and know what camp they run in by their hair style, clothing, and even the charismatic buzz words they often use. Selah!

We are all invited in this 3ʳᵈ day to partake of the revelation that is being served at His celebration. At this feast, He is revealing the Christ. At this celebration, we are conforming to His image, looking like Him, not some system with man-made doctrines and traditions. It is not about wearing clothing or throwing around cliché's that identifies us with some watered-down movement of the past, or, sadly to say, the present. God is raising up a people who are committed to His reputation, not theirs. He is raising up a people who live their lives by His principles and according to His purpose, not their own. He is raising up a people who have received the mark of distinction and who live their lives to please Him and not man.

And finally, He is raising up a people who still and will continue to truly reverence Him, His gifts and His house, a people who have a wholesome dread of displeasing Him. *Thank God there are those that STILL wrap their lives, families and jobs around the Kingdom of God, His plans and purposes.*

The table has been set; revelation is present and being revealed to those who have an ear to hear. Many have been called!

*"For many are called, but few [are] chosen,"* (Matt. 22:14).

Called to what? To preach the gospel of the kingdom!

*"And this gospel of the kingdom shall be preached in all the world for a witness unto all nations; and then shall the end come,"* (Matt. 24:14).

The word *called* in the above verse is the Greek word *"kletos"* (pronounced *klay-tos*), which describes "someone called to an office, someone divinely selected and appointed." Many have been called by God to preach these truths and declare the gospel of the kingdom to a people, church, city, region and world that has become lethargic, cold, indifferent, and apathetic to the things of God. Why are the *few chosen struggling* responding to the call? Because it *will* and *has* cost them everything to declare these truths in the face of religious, glaring opposition. Many ministers that I know personally have lost mates, friends, buildings, property and positions (in the religious community) because of their unwavering stand to declare truth in a watered-down, complacent, seeker-friendly, half-baked system.

*"Ephraim, he hath mixed himself among the people; Ephraim is a cake not turned,"* (Hos. 7:8).

NOW is not the time to let little Johnny's Sunday baseball tournament keep you away from the table. NOW is not the time to let your after-work party keep you away from the table. NOW is not the time to let you're just showed up; unexpected family members or in-laws keep you away from the table (Bring them). NOW is not the time to allow your flesh or emotions to keep you away from the table. NOW is not the time for your favorite weekly TV series to keep you away from the table (after all, today just about anyone has the ability to record their program to be seen at a later time). Have we forgotten the Hebrews writer's admonishment to us?

*"Not forsaking the assembling of ourselves together, as the manner of some [is]; but exhorting [one another]; and so much the more, as ye see the day approaching,"* (Heb. 10:25).

Let me paraphrase this verse from the original language:

"God forbid that we should abandon or desert the corporate assembly of the ekklesia, that time when we come together in one place. There are some introducing the concept that this is no longer important or needed. My instruction is this: Come together more often, even to a greater degree, especially when you discern the seasons changing," (Heb. 10:25, Apostle Hughes paraphrase).

Men and women of God, we have been called in this hour to proclaim the gospel of the kingdom as a witness to the entire world. The word *witness* carries the meaning of "someone or something with evidence." God wants to demonstrate through us these truths to change the world. Remember: Scripture says that He confirms His word with signs following (one translation says with signs accompanying).

*"And they went forth, and preached everywhere, he Lord working with [them], and confirming the word with signs following,"* (Mark 16:20).

Believers don't follow signs; signs are a part of our DNA as CHRISTians. Signs follow, they accompany us. I am not trying to be crude here; however, when a husband and wife have been intimate, there is EVIDENCE. When you and I have been intimate with the Father, there is evidence. The gospel of the kingdom, when preached, will manifest an evidence that the world desperately needs to see.

## Chapter Nine Reflections

How does this parable speak and/or apply to me?

_____

_____

_____

_____

_____

_____

_____

_____

_____

_____

_____

_____

_____

Action Steps:

What actions should I take today, this week, this month to apply these
principles?

_____

_____

_____

_____

_____

_____

_____

_____

_____

_____

_____

_____

_____

Date/Time that these actions were completed?

_____

_____

_____

_____

_____

_____

_____

_____

_____

_____

Closure:

Thoughts, feelings and emotions from these completed actions?

_____

_____

_____

_____

_____

_____

_____

_____

_____

_____

_____

_____

_____

_____

_____

_____

_____

_____

# Chapter Ten

# The Ten Virgins

IN THIS CHAPTER, we will look closely at a parable that has been used by most evangelical ministries predominately referencing the condition of those in the church prior to an any-minute rapture. In this kingdom parable, Jesus refers to ten virgins. The number 10 represents *testimony*, law and *responsibility*. Each of us has the *responsibility* to pursue the presence of God for ourselves. We should all have a *testimony* produced by passing the *test*.

*"Then shall the kingdom of heaven be likened unto ten virgins, which took their lamps, and went forth to meet the bridegroom. And five of them were wise, and five [were] foolish. They that [were] foolish took their lamps, and took no oil with them: But the wise took oil in their vessels with their lamps. While the bridegroom tarried, they all slumbered and slept. And at midnight there was a cry made, Behold, the bridegroom cometh; go ye out to meet him. Then all those virgins arose, and trimmed their lamps. And the foolish said unto the wise, give us of your oil; for our lamps are gone out. But the wise answered, saying, [Not so]; lest there be not enough for us and you: but go ye rather to them that sell, and buy for yourselves. And while they went to buy, the bridegroom came; and they that were ready went in with him to the marriage: and the door was shut. Afterwards came also the other virgins, saying, Lord, Lord, open to us. But he answered and said, Verily I say unto you, I know you not. 13 Watch therefore, for ye know neither the day nor the hour wherein the Son of man cometh,"* (Matt. 25:1-13).

The word *virgin* is the Greek word *"parthenos"* (pronounced *par-then-os*), which describes one who has abstained from uncleanness and whoredoms, one who is chaste. Being a third-generation minister, I have seen many who have abstained from the external acts of what we used to refer to as great sins (adultery, fornication, etc.) only to see them operate in prejudice, racism, hatred, unforgiveness, gossip, unbelief, slander, discord and the like. (Remember: whatever is not of faith is sin, Rom. 14:23.) On Sunday, they wear the right clothes, they drive the right car, they sing in the choir, they teach a class, they amen the preacher, BUT INWARDLY...

*"Beware of false prophets, which come to you in sheep's clothing, but inwardly they are ravening wolves,"* (Matt. 7:15).

These speak against God's anointed forgetting His command to us:

*"[Saying], Touch not mine anointed, and do my prophets no harm,"* (1 Chron.16:22).

*"[Saying], Touch not mine anointed, and do my prophets no harm,"* (Ps. 105:15).

Again, the third scripture proclaiming the exact thing – three times, same warning – MUST be vitally important.

*"The LORD forbid that I should stretch forth mine hand against the LORD'S anointed,"* (1 Sam. 26:11a).

They speak evil of dignities:

*"But chiefly them that walk after the flesh in the lust of uncleanness, and despise government. Presumptuous [are they], selfwilled, they are not afraid to speak evil of dignities,"* (2 Pet. 2:10).

*"Likewise also these [filthy] dreamers defile the flesh, despise dominion, and speak evil dignities,"* (Jude 1:8).

These types of people live by *preference*, NOT *conviction*. Their conscience has been seared.

Also, remember the word virgin is NOT just a reference to a woman. All ten virgins had lamps, which is the Greek word *"lampas"* (pronounced *lam-pas*). This word references a torch or flame fed by oil. It also speaks of guidance. Each of us in God's kingdom has an internal lamp that is fueled/fed by our relationship with Holy Spirit.

The KINGDOM of Heaven is Like 97

Proverbs speaks clearly of this: *"The spirit of man [is] the candle of the LORD, searching all the inward parts of the belly,"* (20:27). (*Candle* is translated as *lamp*.)

Our candle/lamp lights our whole body. That oil which produces illumination comes out of our relations ship with Holy Spirit.

### No relationship = No oil = No illumination!

*"No man, when he hath lighted a candle, putteth [it] in a secret place, neither under a bushel, but on a candlestick, that they which come in may see the light. The light of the body is the eye: therefore when thine eye is single, they whole body is also full of light; but when [thine eye] is evil, they body also [is] full of darkness. Take heed therefore that the light which is in thee be not darkness. If thy whole body therefore [be] full of light, having no part dark, the whole shall be full of light, as when the bright shining of a candle doth give thee light,"* (Luke 11:33-36).

In Luke's gospel, Jesus went on to rebuke the Pharisees for being more concerned about outward appearance than dealing with what is inward. Basically, He was saying that they could fool people with their *external show*, yet He knew what was happening *within*.

*"And the Lord said unto him, Now do ye Pharisees make clean the outside of the cup and the platter; but your inward part is full of ravening and wickedness,"* (Luke 11:39).

Matthew's gospel is more explicit in Jesus' words to the Pharisees:

*"Woe unto you, scribes and Pharisees, hypocrites! For ye make clean the outside of the cup and of the platter, but within they are full of extortion and excess. [Thou} blind Pharisee, cleanse first that [which is] within the cup and platter, that outside of them may be clean also. 27 Woe unto you, scribes and Pharisees, hypocrites! for ye are like unto whited sepulchers, which indeed appear beautiful outward, but are within full of dead [men's] bones, and of all uncleanness. 28 Even so ye also outwardly appear righteous unto men, but within ye are full of hypocrisy and iniquity,"* (Matt. 23:25-28).

Back in our parable, verse 2 brings a division among the ten virgins. Five were labeled *wise* and five were called *foolish*. The Greek word for *wise* identifies an individual who mind perceives and understands and, thus, judges correctly. The Greek word for *foolish* is *"moros"* (pronounced *mo-ros*), which translates as an individual who is impious (irreverent) and godless. Because this person is irreverent and godless, the purpose, counsel and will of God remains hidden and a mystery to them.

There are those in God's house who perceive and understand the times in which we live; however, there are also many who attend church, and yet live irreverent and godless lives. They know *about* God; yet have no intimate relationship *with* Him.

Externally (outwardly), these "ten virgins" appeared to be the same; yet, five had wisdom from within. They had made provision; they had a divine resource within. In verse 3, the King James Bible states that the *foolish took their lamps and took no oil with them*. Outwardly, they looked like the typical "I-go-to-church every Sunday, Wednesday and weekly prayer meeting Christian." They had their lamps (external) things with them, but were missing the main ingredient, oil. The lamps purpose is useless without the oil. The oil feeds the lamp, thus producing the illumination.

Today's church is full of empty lamps, going through the motions, with the purpose, counsel and will of God always just out of reach (and some of these people don't seem to care). Notice very closely this phrase in verse 4: *"the wise took oil **in their vessels** with their **lamps**"* (bold added for emphasis). The oil was in their vessel (first). The word vessel defines as a receptacle or reservoir. Remember what Paul wrote to the Corinthian church:

*"But we have this treasure in earthen vessels, that the excellency of the power may be of God, and not of us,"* (2 Cor. 4:7).

The vessel feeds the lamp; when there is nothing in the vessel, there will be nothing in the lamp. How full is our reservoir? Are you prepared for the seasons ahead? As Jesus continues teaching this parable, He states that the *bridegroom tarried* (see verse 5). The word *tarried* can be translated as "waiting for the next season." The bridegroom was preparing for the next appearing, the next manifestation and the next season. All ten virgins slumbered and slept in the transition. Even the mature ones have moments (even though short-lived; yet, many would never admit it) of lethargy or mediocrity. Some of the phrases used to define the words slumbered and slept are "to be overcome; to become negligent; one yielded to slothfulness or indifference."

All will have their moment, but the wise shake themselves out of slumber. That famous line from the movie *Lion King* roars WITHIN them: REMEMBER WHO YOU ARE!

Let me be very open and transparent right here. I have now been in the ministry forty-three years at the revising of this book. I have had moments, even seasons of great disappointment, discouragement and have asked the proverbial question (I might add, more than once) "Is this really worth it, the cost seems too great, have I ever made an impact on anyone, no one really cares, etc.?"

The indifference sets in, your prayer and study life are affected, and you are now the robot-pastor/minister/leader, going through the motions, just doing your job. Remember, it's not a job, it's an adventure! Then seemingly out of nowhere comes an email, a call, someone coming up after service revealing that your life has greatly impacted theirs, a message preached has changed their life, changed their mindset, brought healing to their marriage, helped prosper their business. Sometimes it's your Father in the faith or prophet friend calling you with spiritual discernment, a word of knowledge or wisdom or at times, even a rebuke saying "What are you doing, shake yourself, get over it" and things that I can't write in this book. SELAH!

Then an "and suddenly" happens and you remember who you are – you come to yourself. It you had quit Sunday after service, you re-hire yourself Monday and you get back to Kingdom business, the Father's work. If the Lord tarries and I leave this earthly house, I want to be remembers as one who didn't quit.

As the rest of the parable unfolds, we see a *clear division* being made. I believe the five wise represent the TRUE church and the five foolish speak of those who are *professors of Christ, NOT possessors of Christ*. I find it interesting that the cry went out at midnight (see verse 6). In those midnight seasons, you can and will really find out what is IN a person. As a Christian, you will share your life and testimony, and you will have experiences with people around you. However, you walk and work out your OWN salvation.

*"Wherefore, my beloved, as ye have always obeyed, not as in my presence only, but now much more in my absence, work out your own salvation with fear and trembling,"* (Phil. 2:12).

Someone once said "unreadiness is the height of folly." Five were unprepared! *Lamps were personal property; each and every individual was and is responsible for the preparation and filling of their own lamp, their own personal relationship with the oil giver.* In *verse 8*, the foolish virgins stated that their lamps had gone out. The Greek word for *gone out* is *"sbennumi"* (pronounced *shen-noo-mee*) and describes something or someone who had *quenched their divine influence.*

Who is quenching your flame?

SEPARATE YOURSELVES FROM THEM TODAY!

What is quenching your flame? RELEASE IT TODAY!

The five wise said to the five foolish, *"Go to them that sell and buy for yourselves"* (verse 9). The word *sell* speaks prophetically of a tradesman. The word "buy" refers to a public assembly and prophetically I believe represents the CHURCH. The five wise were revealing that their reservoir was filled by the tradesman (Apostle, Prophet, Evangelist, Pastor, and Teacher) through the corporate gathering of the Ekklesia, the church.

The five wise virgins were READY (See verse 10) for the celebration; they were ready for intimacy. They were ready for covenant living. The word *ready* is interesting in the Greek language. It is the Greek word *"hetoimos"* (pronounced *het-oy-mos*), which comes from an old noun, *"heteos"* which translates as *fitness.* It describes someone who is spiritually fit, prepared; one who is doing. I believe it represents those busy with the Father's business, those occupying until He comes.

*"And he called his ten servants, and delivered them ten pounds, and said unto them, Occupy till I come,"* (Luke 19:13).

Verse 10 describes the door being shut. The door reveals the entrance, the passageway into the kingdom. The door of the kingdom denotes the conditions that MUST be met in order to be received into the kingdom. What or whom is obstructing your entrance into the kingdom? Don't let anyone or anything keep you from meeting the conditions required to operate in God's kingdom. The traditions of men, man-made doctrines, old wine skins, old though patterns to name just a few will cause you not to see, let alone experience the Kingdom of God. In the final verses (11-13) of this parable, I see a sifting, a separation taking place. The time of outward profession, the time of rituals and symbols void of OIL, LIGHT and POWER is OVER! Verse 13 is not just a reference to some future end-time event. The work *cometh* is the Greek word *"erchomai"* (pronounced *er-khom-ahee*) and describes an appearing, one coming into public view. Where is Christ? In you! He continually desires to be seen, to make His appearance *in us* and *through us* to this world:

*"Ye are the light of the world. A city that is set on an hill cannot be hid,"* (Matt. 5:14).

*"To whom God would make known what [is] the riches of the glory of this mystery among the Gentiles; which is Christ in you, the hop of glory,"* (Col. 1:27).

He desires to pour *you* out a blessing to humanity. Keep the oil flowing; the greatest appearing and illumination is yet to be revealed and seen by all.

## Chapter Ten Reflections

How does this parable speak and/or apply to me?

_____

_____

_____

_____

_____

_____

_____

_____

_____

_____

_____

Action Steps:

What actions should I take today, this week, this month to apply these principles?

_____

_____

_____

_____

_____

_____

_____

_____

_____

_____

_____

_____

_____

_____

Date/Time that these actions were completed?

_____

_____

_____

_____

_____

_____

_____

_____

_____

Closure:

Thoughts, feelings and emotions from these completed actions?

_____

_____

_____

_____

_____

_____

_____

_____

_____

_____

_____

_____

_____

_____

_____

_____

_____

_____

# Chapter Eleven

# The Talents

THIS KINGDOM PARABLE deals with God's servants advancing His kingdom on earth. The word *servant* is interesting in the Greek language. It is the word *"doulos"* (pronounced *doo-los*), which describes "a slave; one who gives himself up to another's will; those whose service is used by Christ in extending and advancing His kingdom cause among men; one devoted to another to the disregard of one's own interest." Heaven's goods (i.e., substance, possessions, wealth and property) have been distributed to God's servants (you and me) for the furtherance of His plans and purpose. In this parable, the Lord distributed the talents with five going to one, two going to another, and one to the last.

*"For [the kingdom of heaven is] as a man traveling into a far country, [who] called his own servants, and delivered unto them his goods. And unto one he gave five talents, to another two, and to another one; to every man according to his several ability; and straightway took his journey. The he that had received the five talents went and traded with the same, and made [them] other five talents. And likewise he that [had received] two, he also gained other two. But he that had received one went and digged in the earth, and hid his lord's money. After a long time the lord of those servants cometh, and reckoned with them. And so he that had received five talents came brought other five talents, saying, Lord, thou hast deliveredst unto me five talents: behold, I have gained beside them five talents more. His lord said unto him, well done, [thou] good and faithful servant; thou has been faithful over a few things, I will make thee ruler over many things: enter thou into the joy of thy lord. He also that had received two talents came and said, Lord, thou deliveredst unto me two talents: behold, I have gained two other talents beside them. His lord said unto him, well done, good and faithful*

*servant; thou hast been faithful over a few things, I will make thee ruler over many things: enter thou into the joy of thy lord. Then he which had received the one talent came and said, Lord, I knew thee that thou art an hard man, reaping where thou has not sown, and gathering where thou hast not strawed: And so I afraid, went and hid they talent in the earth: lo, [there] thou hast [that is] thine. His lord answered and said unto him, [Thou] wicked and slothful servant, thou knewest that I reap where I sowed not, and gather where I have not strawed: Thou oughtest therefore to have put my money to the exchangers, and [then] at my coming I should have received mine own with usury. Take therefore the talent from him, and give [it] unto him which hath ten talents. For unto every one that hath shall be given, and he shall have abundance: but from him that hath not shall be taken away even that which he hath. And cast ye the unprofitable servant into out darkness: there shall be weeping and gnashing of teeth,"* (Matt. 25:14-30).

We MUST understand that we differ from each other only in the amount of gifts received. There has been way too much competition in the Body of Christ concerning these truths. The reason that we differ in gifts has nothing to do with our looks, what kind of cars we drive, where we buy our clothes, our personalities, our locations/positions in the body of Christ, or even our educational status, for that matter. In verse 15, the Amplified Bible say that He gave "to each in proportion to His own personal ability."

A quick side note right here: There is a vast difference between the "*doma*" (Greek word for gifts) gifts that rule stated in Ephesians chapter four and the "*charisma*" (Greek word for gifts) given in Romans chapter twelve (that is another message that I teach to leaders).

*"Wherefore he saith, When he ascended up on high, he led captivity captive, and gave gifts* (Greek "doma") *unto men,"* (Eph. 4:8).

These *doma* gifts are listed in verse 11.

*"And he gave some, apostles; and some, prophets; and some, evangelists; and some, pastors and teachers;"* (Eph. 4:11).

These *charisma* gifts are listed in these verses in Romans.

*"So we, [being] many, are one in body in Christ, and every one member one of another. Having then gifts* (Greek "charisma") *differing according to*

*the grace that is given to us, whether prophecy, [let us prophesy] according to the proportion of faith; Or ministry, [let us wait] on [our] ministering: or he that teacheth, on teaching; Or he that exhorteth, on exhortation: he that giveth, [let him do it] with simplicity; he that ruleth, with diligence; he that sheweth mercy, with cheerfulness. [Let} love be without dissimulation. Abhor that which is evil; cleave to that which is good. [Be] kindly affectioned one to another with brotherly love; in honour preferring one another; Not slothful in business; fervent in spirit; serving the Lord; Rejoicing in hope; patient in tribulations; continuing instant in prayer; Distributing to the necessity of saints; given to hospitality. Bless them which persecute you: bless, and curse not. Rejoice with them that do rejoice, and weep with them that weep,"* (Rom. 12:5-15).

When *charisma* gifts try to rule (don't get hung up on this word, I'm not speaking of dictatorship) like *doma* gifts...stuff happens. (For an in-depth study of this, order my series *The Order of Apostolic Ministry*).

Remember: God made us, so He knows us better than anyone. He knows what talents suit us, He know what we need and what we can handle, and He knows what gifts to give us to be the most effective in His kingdom. The bottom line is *Father* KNOWS *Best* (like the old black and white TV series). We are all pieces of the puzzle, we all have a part in His master plan. He connects us to whom He desires; we are not complete without each other. When we are IN PLACE, the full potential of the puzzle (picture, vision) is realized. As long as we are all producing according to the gift's He gave us, then we are successful and in His will.

### A Personal Example

Once during a service that I was ministering in, I threw a thousand-piece Thomas Kincade puzzle out into the congregation as a prophetic gesture. There were pieces on the floor, in chairs, in people's hair and on their clothes. I then ran out into the congregation and began picking up one piece of the puzzle at a time and compared it to the picture on the front of the box.

As I was doing this illustration, I was asking that church a question: "How come this piece of the puzzle doesn't look like the picture on the box?" The answer was simple, yet profound! The one piece wasn't complete because it wasn't connected, it hadn't been *fitly framed together* (see Eph. 4:16). The other thing I stated was that each piece of the puzzle (vision) didn't get to *choose* who it was connected to. That was prearranged by the designer of the picture (vision).

Without this understanding, the church has experienced entirely too much self-inflicted pain trying to remove ourselves from those that God has connected to us. We have tried to fit our piece of the puzzle into a shape, form or system that we weren't designed to fit into. Once the church finally realizes that this is all part of God's process, we will then quit *"kicking against the pricks"* (see Acts 9:5). At that point, understanding the plans and purpose of God, hopefully, once and for all, we will stop resisting and unknowingly being used of the enemy to cause more pain and division. At the re-writing of this book, there are people in that church that still carry around their piece of the puzzle as a reminder.

The Apostle Paul reiterates these truths in his writing to the Corinthian Church:

*"But the manifestation of the Spirit is given to every man to profit withal. For to one is given by the Spirit the work of wisdom; to another the word of knowledge by the same Spirit; To another faith by the same Spirit; to another the gifts of healing by the same Spirit; To another the working of miracles; to another prophecy; to another discerning of spirits; to another [divers] kinds of tongues; to another the interpretation of tongues: But all these worketh that one and the selfsame Spirit, dividing to every man severally as he will,"* (1 Cor. 12:7-11).

In verse 11, The King James Version uses the word *severally*, which is the Greek word *"idios"* (pronounced *id-ee-os*), which simply translates as "their own." Jesus is the dispenser of gifts, and He gives everyone their own as He wills. That is why we should never covet our brother's gifts and talents; they don't FIT us.

Jesus gives gifts unto men: *"Wherefore he saith, When he ascended up on high, he led captivity captive, and gave gifts unto men,"* (Eph. 4:8).

*"And he gave some, apostles; and some, prophets; and some, evangelists; and some, pastors and teachers; For the perfecting of the saints, for the work*

*of the ministry, for the edifying of the body of Christ: Till we all come in the unity of faith, and of the knowledge of the Son of God, unto a perfect man, unto the measure of the stature of the fullness of Christ: That we [henceforth] be no more children, tossed to and fro, and carried about with every wind of doctrine, by the sleight of men, [and] cunning craftiness, whereby they lie in wait to deceive; But speaking the truth in love, may we grow up into him in all things, which is the head, [even] Christ,"* (Eph.4:8, 11-15).

These gifts are given for the perfecting of the saints. The word *perfecting* describes one who is "fully equipped and completely furnished." You can't launch yourself into the work of the ministry without those gifts equipping and preparing you for what lies ahead. We have had enough shipwrecks and faith failures. Without proper equipping, we can end up tossed to and fro. This translates as someone who is agitated mentally, like wave after wave beating against you. There are those who ignorantly proclaim today that the gifts (prophet, apostle, etc.) aren't needed any more, or even worse, no longer exist. I thank God for the ministry gifts and spiritual fathers that God has put in my life to keep me on the right track and away from funky doctrines.

Notice in Matthew 25:16 the word *traded* in our parable. It is the Greek word *"ergazomai"* (pronounced *er-gad-zom-ahee*), which refers to a person who "worked, labored, did business, made gains by trading, produced and acquired." The man who *traded* was producing with his lord's talents. By the way, they are the Lord's talents; we are simply the stewards of them. God's plan is simple: REPRODUCE!

The first servant was given five talents. He doubled them, producing ten, and the next servant had two talents and double them, producing four. The servant who had one talent…Well! Everything God gives us is designed to produce, expand, enlarge, grow and DOUBLE. At times, when we have missed it, and we all have, when it seems like failure, God CAN and WILL turn it around for us. Here are some scriptural examples:

*"And the Lord turned the captivity of Job, when he prayed for his friends: also the LORD gave Job twice as much as he had before,"* (Job 42:10). The Hebrew word for *gave* translates like this: "added all that had been to Job unto the double." As Joyce Meyer says, "Double for your trouble!"

*"If the theft be certainly found in his hand alive, whether it be ox, or ass, or sheep; he shall restore double,"* (Exod. 22:4).

*"If a man shall deliver unto his neighbor money or stuff to keep, and it be stolen out of the man's house; if the thief be found, let him pay double,"* (Exod. 22:7).

*"And it came to pass, when they were gone over, that Elijah said unto Elisha, Ask what I shall do for thee, before I be taken away from thee. And Elisha said, I pray thee, let a double portion of thy spirit be upon me. And he said, Thou hast asked a hard thing: [nevertheless], if thou see e [when I am] taken from thee, it shall be so unto thee; but if not, it shall not be [so],"* (2 Kings 2:9-10).

*"Speak ye comfortably to Jerusalem, and cry unto her, that her warfare is accomplished, that her iniquity is pardoned: for she hath received of the LORD"S hand double for all her sins,"* (Isa.40:2).

*"For your shame [ye shall have] double; and [for] confusion they shall rejoice in their portion: therefore in their land they shall possess the double: everlasting joy shall be unto them,"* (Isa. 61:7).

*"Let the elders that rule well be counted worthy of double honour, especially they who labour in the word and doctrine,"* (1 Tim. 5:17).

God desires that His servants who use their gifts/talents wisely for Him receive DOUBLE.

How do we *gain* for the Father? The word *gain* in the original language give us that very insight. The Greek word for *gain* is *"kerdaino"* (pronounced *ker-dah-ee-no*) and depicts someone gaining from "shunning and gain escaping evil." God's way/path/road is prosperous, healthy and blessed. Stay the course; stay on course. The Master pays well.

In verse 18 of Matthew 25, this kingdom parable gives a picture of someone who went down the wrong path. By the way, the number 18 in the Bible represents bondage. Wrong choices and wrong uses of our gifts will lead to bondage. This servant *hid* (Greek work *"apokrupto,"* pronounced *ap-ok-roop-to*), means "concealed and kept secret his talent."

## Another Personal Example

I most definitely understand the word *hid* mentioned above. In 1988, during a week of separation, prayer and fasting, God spoke to me as clearly as I had ever heard him up until that day. He spoke concerning the gift of the Apostle; and stated that I was called to and would stand in, operate and function in that Ephesians 4 gift. In 1988, in the circle that I was involved with, there was no one (that I knew) speaking in any real depth concerning apostolic and prophetic ministry, or apostles and prophets. I was frightened; none of my ministry friends were preaching, teaching or even communicating amongst each other concerning these offices. I was afraid of being removed from the ministry fellowships that I was a part of; I was afraid of being labeled *weird, a flake,* or worse. I was concerned that even those closest to me in ministry would not understand, and thus, reject me. I had not yet been delivered from the face of men.

*"Ye shall not respect persons in judgment; [but] ye shall hear the small as well as the great; ye shall not be afraid of the face of man; for the judgment [is] God's: and the cause that is too hard for you, bring [it] unto me, and I will hear it,"* (Deut. 1:17).

I didn't speak of that encounter to a soul, literally for years. It wasn't until the late 1990s that a prophet friend of mine, Wynn Hinson (three weeks later, on Father's Day morning, he went home to be with the Lord), confronted me as we were grilling steaks outside one evening. He turned and looked me directly in my eyes and said, "Why are you running from your calling?" I played dumb (and that wasn't the first time I've manifested that spirit) and said, "What are you talking about Wynn?" He didn't mince words; he said, "You know exactly what I am talking about, the gift of the apostle. Are you still concerned about and fearful what people will think?"

That day I promised the Lord and Prophet Wynn Hinson that no matter the cost (and believe me, there has been more than I have time to pen here), I would obey the call. Within the next several months, more than one confirmation came, from more than one source, some that I knew and through some I didn't. Since that day, because of the Lord's gifting and calling, and my obedience (well, at times), I have pioneered ministries, ministered in apostolic and prophetic conferences, not only in the States, but also in Seoul,

Korea; Ozamiz City, Philippines; Ekpoma, (Edo State) Nigeria; and Nakuru, (Nairobi) Kenya, as well as Mexico with many new opportunities and launches in front of me as I re-write this book. I have written five books, working on my 6th, established businesses to further God's plan for my and ministry, as well as raising up spiritual sons and daughters to far surpass anything that I have done or may ever do in the kingdom of God.

As you read this, can you relate? Has God spoken to you concerning your gift? Have you tried to share with family or even close friends what you believe concerning your gift, calling or talents only to be rejected or criticized? Don't let them talk you out of your calling! Remember, the Apostle Paul wrote in the book of Acts to "...*obey God rather than men.*" (Acts 5:29) Your blessing comes from and through God, not man.

The servant who *hid* the one talent can represent many within the body of Christ today: afraid of the people and what they will say, not wanting *that gift* but someone else's, abusing the gift/talent and using it for the wrong motive, etc. The servant told his lord that he "*hid thy talent in the earth,*" (Matt. 25:25). I find it interesting that the servant hid the talent in the earth. What are we made of? EARTH! This represents the individual who consumes his talent/gift upon his own flesh, one who uses and abuses it for fleshly gain with wrong or impure motives. It goes on to say in verse 18 that he hid his lord's money.

The Greek word for *money* is "*argurion*" (pronounced *ar-goo-ree-on*), which translates as silver. What does silver speak of? REDEMPTION! Our Redemption is not just for us. It is not to be hidden; it is to be revealed to mankind and seen operating in our lives before the world. We are to be a witness (someone or something with evidence)! What and why are you hiding it? Release the fear!

The servants that produced for their Lord were called *good and faithful* servants. *Good* is a reference to one who is useful and faithful. It refers to an individual who is faithful in business transactions, one who is faithful in the execution of commands and in the discharge of official duties. In other words, one who can be relied upon. Remember: The talents are the Lord's; He made us stewards of them. It is better to come in LAST in faithfulness than FIRST in unfaithfulness. You don't *lose* what you *use.* It is pathetic when people get in fear of losing what they WILL NOT USE! Of course, we are unalike in the gifts and talents that Father has given us; we must all be alike in our obedience to use what God has given each of us.

In verse 24, the servant begins to lie and speak against his lord. He wasn't a hard man, and he didn't reap where he hadn't sown. This servant is now on the defensive; he is speaking against the very one who gave to him to begin with. When you become defensive, you move off the offensive, you are no longer advancing, you are retreating. The lord called this servant "...wicked and slothful..." The Greek words for these describe an individual who has produced their own hardships. They are being harassed from their own sluggishness and hesitation, so they end up diseased and blind (spiritually).

Verse 30 ends this parable by casting the unprofitable servant into the outer darkness. These words are very unattractive in the Greek language. *Unprofitable* translates as "useless or good for nothing" and the words, *outer darkness* as "outside the region of light." No one wants to be outside of God's light. It is the illumination, the revelation, the light of God's Word that can and will keep us from falling into darkness and losing our way.

Your talents/gifts are GOD-GIVEN and must be used for His glory. Each of us is designed to produce fruit; each of us is created to manifest a return on His giving. Begin to declare that His will through His gifts will be done in and through your life.

## Chapter Eleven Reflections

How does this parable speak and/or apply to me?

_____

_____

_____

_____

_____

_____

_____

_____

_____

_____

_____

Actions Steps:

What actions should I take today, this week, this month to apply these principles?

_____

_____

_____

_____

_____

_____

_____

_____

_____

_____

_____

_____

_____

Date/Time that these actions were completed?

_____

_____

_____

_____

_____

_____

_____

_____

_____

_____


Closure:

Thoughts, feelings and emotions from these completed actions?

_____

_____

_____

_____

_____

_____

_____

_____

_____

_____

_____

_____

_____

_____

_____

_____

# Chapter Twelve

# The Laborers

THIS IS A hard-hitting look into the kingdom of God, and an unveiling of *where* folks are and *what* they are doing for the householder. The word *householder* defines as "the good man or master of the house." In essence; it is a reference to the Lord. You and I have been *hired* (Greek word "*misthoo*," pronounced *mis-tho-o*) by the Lord to work in His vineyard. The word *hired* describes and individual who has rewards or dues coming to him/her because of their labor.

*"For the kingdom of heaven is like unto a man [that is] an householder, which went out early in the morning to hire labourers into his vineyard. And when he had agreed with the labourers for a penny a day, he sent them into his vineyard. And he went out about the third hour, and saw other standing idle in the marketplace,"* (Matt. 20:1-3).

These are rewards which God will present to those whose good deeds and endeavors have come up before Him. We all have been promised wages (blessings). Both natural and spiritual; now all of us have been released to *occupy* until the Goodman returns (Luke 19:13).

On a side note, I find interesting the daily amount agreed upon between the householder (Lord) and the laborer (you and I). A penny a day! The Roman penny was the eight part of an ounce, which equals about fourteen cents ($0.14). The number 14 in biblical numeric's symbolizes salvation. Each and every one of us is *working out* our own salvation on a daily basis, (Phil. 2:12). The words *work out* in Philippians characterize an individual who works to get results, one who labors doing ministry business, thus acquiring and gaining through his/her employment.

I believe that great prophetic insight is revealed in verse 3 of this parable. Jesus taught that during the 3rd hour (see my book *The Third Day* for more insight), the householder went into the marketplace and found people standing idle. The word *idle* is definitely a word of rebuke. It indicates any individual who is "slow in their work; barren; one who has a *free from work mindset;* one who works at their own leisure; lazy; or simply one who shuns (avoids; shrinks back from) the labor they ought to be performing as agreed upon at their hire.

Where are these idle people? In the marketplace! This word *marketplace* has a much broader meaning than you may think. It refers to an assembly, especially of people. It includes the place of elections, the place of buying and selling, and any place people congregate. The church is in its 3rd-day season; we are taking the *gospel of the kingdom* to the world (marketplace) for a witness (something or someone with evidence).

*"And this gospel of the kingdom shall be preached in all the world for a witness unto all nations; and then shall come the end,"* (Matt. 24:14).

This is the time for keeping our hands on the plow, pressing forward, laboring in the marketplace, NOT loitering (just hanging around), by the way, in many places of business, it is against the law to loiter. In verse 4, the Word of the Lord rings loud and clear: GO!

*"And said unto them; Go ye also into the vineyard, and whatsoever is right I will give you. And they went their way,"* (Matt. 20:4).

Throughout the scriptures, there are many references where this truth rings loud and clear:

*"And he said unto them, Go ye into all the world, and preach the gospel to every creature,"* (Mark 16:15).

*"Go ye therefore into the highways, and as many as ye shall find, bid to marriage,"* (Matt. 22:9).

*"And the lord said unto the servant, Go out into the highways and hedges, and compel [them] to come in, that my house may be filled,'* (Luke 14:23).

Notice closely the next few verses of the parable:

*"Again he went out about the sixth and ninth hour, and did likewise. 6 And about the eleventh hour he went out, and found others standing idle, and saith unto them, Why stand ye here all the day idle?"* (Matt. 20:5-6).

The number 6 represents the number of man (see Gen. 1:31), and the number 9 represents finality, fruit, gifts and birth. The number 11 represents disorder. In this 3$^{rd}$ hour (day), God desires fruit from His people. He has given us gifts (the 5-fold ministry gifts as well as the 9 gifts of the Spirit) to help us birth the destiny that resides on the inside of each and every single one of us. This is a day when the disorder in our lives is being exposed by the light and revelation of God's word. If you are idle in this season, you are probably in disorder. Selah!

God is once again reminding us of the things that are most important, Are His priorities our priorities? Are we sincerely seeking first the kingdom?

*"But seek ye first the kingdom of God, and his righteousness; and all these things shall be added unto you,"* (Matt. 6:33).

I have never seen a time as this when so many in the church operate with such a self-gratifying attitude as in this season. Most do what is convenient where they and/or their families are concerned. Church (especially mid-week Bible study) has become an option, not a priority. Their jobs, the kids' extracurricular activities, needing family time (you really don't want to hear my definition of this one), running every weekend here and there to visit this person and that relative. All of these things and much more now take precedence over corporate worship. But when things get bad, and they usually do, they are the first ones calling for help and really can't explain why they need it (Selah again).

Are you winning souls?

*"The fruit of the righteous [is] a tree of life; and he that winneth souls [is] wise,"* (Prov. 11:30).

Are we restoring the prodigal sons and daughters? (See Luke 15:11-32).

I know of hundreds, if not thousands, of Bible school graduates sitting in churches in the cities where they graduated, waiting for their big break. You know what I mean, waiting for one of the big Christian television networks to recognize them. They are waiting for one of the well-known ministers to ask them to speak at their conference. They are sitting in the marketplace and waiting...waiting...waiting. They have their diplomas, but they are waiting. They have their degrees, but they are waiting. They have their prophetic word, but they are waiting. They are ANOINTED; they can do all things through CHRIST who strengthen them, but they are waiting! I have a word for them: GO!

Where are the pioneers, where are the planters, and where are those who are willing to be led by a compass and not a map? What are we doing for/in the kingdom of God? What does it mean when you hear people say, "I'm just waiting on God?" All too often, it is NOTHING but a religious cliché. Do you remember this scripture?

*"But they that **wait** upon the LORD shall renew [their] strength; they shall mount up with wings as eagles; they shall run and not be weary; [and] they shall walk, and not faint,"* (Isaiah 40:31; bold added for emphasis).

The word *wait* in the above verse doesn't mean to do nothing. It is the Hebrew word *"quvah"* (pronounced *kaw-vaw*), which comes from another word which portrays a servant, a worshipper. It describes what we would refer to as a waiter or waitress. Therefore, those truly *waiting* on God are servants, workers, and worshipers. They are the ones whose strength changes from their own to His (that is how the word *renew* actually defines). They are runners and walkers in His kingdom; they don't easily faint or grow weary.

These graduates are still sitting in a city waiting for some *man* to hire them:

*"They say unto him, because no man hath hired us. He saith unto them, Go ye also into the vineyard; and whatsoever is right, [that] shall he receive,"* (Matt. 20:7).

The householder's response was the same again: GO!

At first, the next verse in this parable was a challenge for me until I began to break it down. My father, Dr. Don Hughes Sr. (passed on to his reward in April, 2015), was greatly responsible for teaching me how to study words in the Bible as well as understanding the law of "first mention" (when something is mentioned first or in a sequence), and one of my spiritual fathers, Bishop

(Dr.) Vernon D Owens (passed on to his reward July 2006), taught me how to see prophetic truths throughout the scriptures:

*So when even was come, the lord of the vineyard saith unto his steward, Call the labourers, and them them [their] hire, beginning from the last unto the first,"* (Matt. 20:8).

Verse 8 states that the *steward* gave to the laborers, not the lord of vineyard. The word for *steward* in the Greek is *"epitropos"* (pronounced *ep-it-rop-os*), which depicts "a tutor; guardian; overseer; one who has the care and tutelage of children." Can you see the prophetic implication here? It is a reference to the man/woman of God that he has placed over you.

Your blessings are ordered of the Lord to be passed through the steward on to the laborer. Like it or not, the release of your blessings are tied to your spiritual leaders…SELAH! Today, many are saying, "I don't need a pastor. Apostles and prophets are no longer needed; they are done away with. I'm my own person; no preacher is going to tell me what to do." Consider your ways! How is that working for you?

The next part of this parable presents another paradigm (pattern) that I see arising within the body of Christ that is a dangerous and destructive force against unity and a "commanded blessing." (See Ps. 133).

*And when they came that [were hired] about the eleventh hour, they received every man a penny. But when the first came, they supposed that they should have received more; and they likewise received every man a penny. And when they had received [it], they murmured against the goodman of the house, Saying, These last have wrought [but] one hour, and thou has made them equal unto us, which have borne the burden and heat of the day.*

*"But he answered one of them, and said, Friend, I do thee no wrong: didst not thou agree with me for a penny? Take [that] thine [is], and go thy way: I will give unto this last, even unto thee. Is it not lawful for me to do what I will with mind own? Is thine eye evil, because I am good?"* (Matt.20:9-15).

In this hour, all of those coming out of disorder, making things right and working in the kingdom have the same rights and blessings as those who have worked from the beginning. This is not the time for jealousy and competition. Whatever happened to "rejoice with them that do rejoice?"

*"Rejoice with them that do rejoice,"* (Rom.12:15a).

Let's look at another scripture which states, when one member is honored, all the members should rejoice with them.

*And whether one member suffer, all the members suffer with it; or one member be honoured, all the members rejoice with it,"* (1Cor.12:26).

In verse 11 of the parable, it states that the first-hired laborers *murmured* against the goodman (Lord) of the house. You know people like this (you could even be one) at church, on the job, and even in your family. The word *murmured* is the Greek word "*gogguzo*" (pronounced *gong-good-zo*), which describes a person who "mutters to themselves and others; to say something in a low tone; those who confer secretly together; those who discontentedly complain."

The religious church is full of the *elder brothers* (see Luke 15), those who reject the restoration of their family members (members by natural and/or spiritual birth). They have a "they don't deserve what I have; I am better than and above them; I would never do what they did; I should get the greater blessing" mentality. We are each rewarded for our OWN labor; your blessing is not based on what *someone else did or how long they have been doing it*. It is based solely on your obedience to your calling, not your hire date.

Jesus' explanation was simple, yet profound: "Friend, I do thee no wrong: didst thou agree with me for a penny?" In other words, I have honored my covenant agreement with you exactly as I promised. His promises are yea and amen and no good thing will He withhold from them who walk uprightly.

*"For all the promises of God in him [are] yea, and in him Amen, unto the glory of God by us,"* (2 Cor.1:20).

*"For the LORD God [is] a sun and shield: the LORD will give grace and glory: no good [thing] will he withhold from them that walk uprightly,"* (Ps. 84:11).

*"And all these blessings shall come on thee, and overtake thee, if thou shalt hearken unto the voice of the LORD thy God,"* (Deut. 28:2).

The goodman of the house asks the laborers a question in verse 15 of the parable: "Is thine eye evil, because I am good?" A more defining way to ask this question would be: "Are you jealous because I am good to those people?" or "Are you envious because I am so generous?"

We must ask ourselves some honest, heartfelt questions: Why would we be upset if our brother or sister were blessed on the same level or to the same degree as us? Does it really matter in the kingdom scheme of things that you "clocked in" a few hours, weeks or months before your brother/sister did? Do you really think that God will love you more than your co-laborers because you have more fruit?

As I have ministered over the years, I have always taught folks to rejoice and be thankful when they see their brother/sister blessed with a raise, promotion, new car, new home, vacation, etc. Why? Because it sets them up to be blessed by keeping their hearts right! God doesn't respect that person more because it is their season for blessing. He is no *respecter of persons*, but He is of *the principles* those persons operate in that bring them into the blessings.

Jesus ends the parable in verse 16 with the statement, *the last shall be first, and the first last: for many be called but few chosen.* Think about it: Some are coming to the forefront in this season; others are passing on as their season has ended. When we come in IS NOT the important thing; what we do while we are here IS.

Every single one of us has a destiny in Him. My destiny will be fulfilled based on what I do, not on what others do or don't do. Jesus Himself stated that the call has gone out to many. We have all heard individuals over the years say, "I'm called." But, how many have you ever heard say, I'm chosen." To be chosen means to be picked out.

I once heard a minister state that the word *chosen* describes someone who has gone through a process, one who had passed the test and proven faithful. There have been literally tens of thousands who have acknowledged the call, only to decide the price too great, the process is too difficult. In over four plus decades of ministry, I have heard the statement countless times, I'm called. I have yet to hear the first person declare, I am chosen!

After reading this book, my prayer for you is three-fold:

1. That you have been *challenged* to think outside the box as I have been in the last several years.

2. That you are always open to *change*; it is necessary for out spiritual growth. We are continually being transformed into His image.

3. And finally that the truths in this book have *blessed* (impacted) your life to the point that you will produce fruit, thirty (30), sixty (60) and one hundred (100) fold in this life.

Lead team member,
Dr. Don D Hughes
REV House, Inc.
Tulsa, Oklahoma
www.revhouse.org

Made in the USA
Columbia, SC
21 January 2019